LIFE IN DANCE

LIFE IN DANCE

DARCEY BUSSELL

WITH JUDITH MACKRELL

ARROW

Published by Arrow Books in 1999

1 3 5 7 9 10 8 6 4 2

Copyright © Darcey Bussell 1998

Darcey Bussell has asserted her right under the Copyright,
Designs and Patents Act, 1988 to be identified as the author of this work

First published in the United Kingdom in 1998 by Century

Arrow Books
The Random House Group Limited
20 Vauxhall Bridge Road, London SW1V 2SA

Random House Australia (Pty) Limited
20 Alfred Street, Milsons Point, Sydney,
New South Wales 2061, Australia

Random House New Zealand Limited
18 Poland Road, Glenfield,
Auckland 10, New Zealand

Random House South Africa (Pty) Limited
Endulini, 5A Jubilee Road,
Parktown 2193, South Africa

The Random House Group Limited Reg. No. 954009
www.randomhouse.co.uk

A CIP catalogue record for this book is available
from the British Library

Papers used by The Random House Group Limited
are natural, recyclable products made from wood grown in
sustainable forests. The manufacturing processes conform to
the environmental regulations of the country of origin

ISBN 0 09 9280221

Typeset by MATS, Southend-on-Sea, Essex
Printed and bound in Germany by
Elsnerdruck, Berlin

ACKNOWLEDGEMENTS

To have someone fit so seamlessly into one's working life is rare. Judith Mackrell, with her knowledge of my career, her understanding and her consideration has made our association so pleasurable. I hope she feels the same!

As always, at the eye of the storm, Janine Limberg is by my side, and I am so appreciative.

I have been so fortunate in my career, and I really wish to thank Sir Kenneth and Lady Deborah MacMillan, Sir Anthony Dowell, Monica Mason, Donald MacLeary and the long list of my ballet friends. When you are forced to reflect upon your experiences, you are reminded of all the help you couldn't have done without. Within the ballet world I would like to thank Mrs Kastrati, Patricia Linton, Nancy Kilgor, Dame Merle Park, Sir Peter Wright, John Browett, Aileen Kelly, Andreas Regueke, Jenny Mills, Lucy Haith, Angela Coia, Jane Paris, Michael Brown, Juan Leirado, Liz Foyster and Betty Anderton. For all those outside, thank you for being such good friends and letting me be me.

Of course, my husband's support has been unfailing.

The last word goes to my parents, my thanks and love to them. They have endured the last thirty years, and I know they will be with me for the rest of my career's ups and downs.

CONTENTS

INTRODUCTION

HOW DO I describe my feelings about ballet? It's what I do every day and it's become my natural element. I can't imagine my world without it and I certainly doubt that I could have succeeded at anything else. When I'm taking my bows after a ballet like *Romeo and Juliet* I feel transported. I'm listening to the applause of over two thousand people, feeling waves of emotion and warmth, and for just a few minutes I feel as if I deserve it all. But when I was a child, no one would ever have said that I was born to dance.

I was quite a clumsy little girl, and my favourite games were playing sports and dressing up. Although I had a tutu I used to wear it with a pair of cowboy boots, and I definitely wasn't fantasizing about being a ballerina.

My mother says she took me to see ballet at the theatre when I was still very small but unlike Anna Pavlova, who felt that she'd discovered her destiny the moment she saw the stage, I can't remember a thing of what we watched.

I even attended ballet classes every Saturday, from the age of about five, but it was something I only agreed to because my friends went. None of us took it very seriously, and certainly no one ever said, 'Oh, she's going to be another little Margot Fonteyn.' In fact sometimes, when my mother came to collect me, I'd have been sitting under the piano for the whole class. I was very stubborn. If I didn't feel like joining in, I wouldn't.

It was only when I was eleven and had begun to attend a stage school that I began to enjoy ballet properly. I discovered that I was good at it and after a year of studying hard I begged to be allowed to audition for White Lodge, The Royal Ballet Junior School. I didn't have much of a training but my examiners must have seen some kind of potential in me because I was accepted. Yet even at The Royal Ballet School it wasn't until I was fourteen that I found in myself a real hunger, a genuine obsession with being a ballerina. And that was partly because everyone thought I was such a disaster.

My first year at the school had gone very badly. Even *I* recognized how far I was behind the others in my class when I first arrived, and when I came to take my exam – the first ballet exam I'd ever attempted – I barely knew what I should be doing. I can still remember my teacher standing on a stool outside the room, watching us through the window, and feeling that this must be one of the worst experiences of my life. After the exam was over I burst into tears because I knew I'd done so badly. But instead of comforting me my teacher was furious. She stormed at me, 'I've never been so embarrassed in my life as watching you.'

I was devastated. I couldn't understand why she was putting me down when I was so upset. Why wasn't she trying to make me feel better? But when she went on to say, 'Maybe ballet just isn't right for you,' I became very, very angry. Her attitude shocked me into a new view of myself, and it was a turning point in my career. Until that moment I'd been feeling sorry for myself, wondering why I wasn't getting more help from anyone, but then I hardened. I was determined to show her, to pay her back, and now I know that she did me a kind of favour, because that gut determination is what every dancer has to find. No one can go into dance and not want it really badly. The hunger has to come from inside. You can't get it from a teacher or from a pushy mother. You have to be really stubborn yourself.

So after that exam I worked and worked, making sure that the next year I passed my exam with Honours. And it wasn't just my technique that improved, it was also my self-discipline, which is another quality dancers cannot do without if they are going to survive.

In dance, our bodies are our instruments and we have to work at them every day. People often ask me how I can put up with the hard work of ballet, the daily drudgery of class and rehearsal, but it becomes an addiction. I now live with a constant feeling of guilt which nags at me if I haven't worked hard enough in the studio, or if my performances haven't been up to standard. I enjoy spotting flaws in my dancing so that I can figure out how to put them right. The whole science of ballet has become completely fascinating to me.

But as well as being physically disciplined, dancers need mental discipline. Ballet pushes us to the edge of who we think we are and we have to learn how to deal with that. Basically, from the moment we begin serious training, nothing is ever good enough. Every time we master a step or perform a good show we need to do it as well – if not better – the next time. We want to be the best, we want to please everyone, but of course every teacher or choreographer has a different idea of what the best is, and we're surrounded by other dancers who also want to succeed. It's only when we get older that we learn to accept the dancers we are, the bodies we are, and the artists we are – and learn to like it.

This is a hard balance to find. Dancers have to be obsessive about ballet, it has to be what they love doing most and what they are most determined to succeed at. But they also have to be able to keep it in proportion. I find that it's just as important for me to be able to cut off and relax as it is to be able to work hard, not only because it allows my body to recover but because it gives me a rest from the pressure. I have to strive to be normal in order to keep the job in proportion. If you let ballet become your whole life you can be so easily hurt because there are so many things that can go wrong. A serious injury can cut your career off at any moment, and of course the career is so short anyway. When I was young I had no sense of how few working years a dancer has; it didn't mean anything to me. But now I'm older it has begun to hit me that I've only got a limited time left and I don't want to waste any of it. I know my body so much better than I did before which not only means that I know my limitations but that I also know what I can do and how I can keep improving. When I perform now I can get to a different level – beyond the purely technical. The wonderful thing about being a dancer is that the craving to get better never leaves you; you are always inspired to find out new things about yourself.

I

FROM BABY TO BUNHEAD: HOW I CAME TO BE A BALLERINA

MY MOTHER, ANDREA, was certainly not a conventional ballet mother, in fact when I first asked her if I could audition for The Royal Ballet School she was completely opposed to the idea. She'd gone to the school herself when she was eleven and it hadn't been a very successful experience for her. Her ballet teacher had rather pushed her into going, and once there she hated the discipline and felt that she didn't fit in. She was disconcerted to discover that if she or one of the other girls didn't sit up straight enough in class a stick would be put down the back of her blouse, and even outside class they were expected to maintain a very proper demeanour. This was totally unnatural for my mother, and she was always being told off for climbing trees, doing backflips on the lawn or taking her gloves off in the train. Her image didn't fit either as her body was very angular and she had short hair. She left after a few years.

By the time I was born in April 1969 she was working as a model and acting in films and she also had her own clothes shop. But she was still only twenty-one when she had me, so as I grew up we were very very close – a little unit. I was always very proud of my mother, she seemed very glamorous and young compared to the mothers of my friends, and we shared a passion for clothes. Even as a toddler I used to change my outfit several times a day and I can still remember how much I loved my purple denim jacket with silver studs. I also had a huge dressing-up box and whenever my friends came round we used to drape ourselves in chiffon and parade up and down the street in high-heeled shoes.

We lived in West London where I was looked after by a lot of different au pair girls. I thought they were all wonderful, particularly a Spanish girl who played the guitar for me while I dressed up as a gypsy and danced around the room. I did a lot of dancing – and running and hopping and jumping – because as soon as I could walk I apparently became wildly hyperactive. My mother says she had to keep reins on me when I was very small because otherwise I'd jump out of the car and run and run and she couldn't catch me.

I was also an only child for the first seven years of my life – and I have to admit I was a spoilt brat. Looking back I only ever remember being refused one thing, which was a little pair of ankle boots which had just come into fashion. I was longing for a pair to wear to school but my mother told me I'd look like an overgrown pixie. But at least I knew, even at the time, that I was spoilt, so I don't think I was mean or selfish with it. And after my mother remarried when I was five, I was thrilled that she went on to give me what I'd always longed for most – a brother and a sister.

Her new husband was Phillip Bussell, a dentist, and as soon as they were married he adopted me straight away. I remember going to court where I was asked if I liked him being my dad. I said, 'Yes I do,' and after that I always regarded him as my father, never as my step-father.

After the wedding the three of us went travelling for a year and, looking back, it seems to have been the perfect way for me to get used to having a father. We drove all around America, which may have inspired my passion for cars; I can still remember how big and shiny American cars seemed to me, and the exciting succession of motels we stayed in. We visited the mountains and the desert, then, after eight months, we went to stay with my grandmother in Sydney.

I went to school there for a few months which I don't remember much of at all. But I *do* remember that my best friend next door had a swimming pool in her garden and that we used to have lunch outdoors every day. This seemed an amazingly carefree way to live, it was so unlike London.

Soon after we returned to England my brother, James, was born. I'm certain that I didn't feel jealous or mind sharing my mother as my memories are all of being thrilled. He was a very beautiful baby with lots of blond curls and he was very calm. His only fault, as far as I was concerned, was refusing to let me dress up his Action Man when he got older – so I was very happy when my sister, Zaylie, was born two years later. She had boxes full of dolls, and I was allowed to dress them up all the time.

Much as I adored James and Zaylie though, it didn't stop me being a horribly annoying child. I was still a show-off and I still always wanted to be centre stage. We used to have guests staying in the house quite often and I'd always rush in to see them first thing in the morning and try to entertain them. My mother had hung large mirrors all around our flat and I went through a phase when I was obsessed with looking at myself. I was constantly trying out different expressions and striking different poses. Maybe it was the performer in me, but it got to the point where I'd be looking at my reflection even while I was talking to someone else. My father got so irritated he threatened to cover every mirror with a sheet unless I stopped doing it, yet I think that was the only time I felt that I'd stepped over a line and been made to feel vain or cocky.

At primary school certainly, I wasn't much of a success – the only things I was good at were art and sports. By that time I'd grown out of being a chubby toddler with a passion for chiffon and had become very athletic. I played in the boys' football team and was very good at keeping possession of the ball because the boys were a bit scared of tackling me. I was also in the rounders team because I could hit the ball so far, and I was very serious about gymnastics and swimming. I won a couple of prizes and for a time I thought about becoming a professional swimmer. But academically I wasn't interested.

Later in my schooling I was diagnosed as suffering from slight dyslexia, but at primary school my teachers just thought I was lazy. I loved art and history, but my spelling was hopeless and I could never finish any of my stories. Of course feeling inadequate made me very naughty in class and I would frequently lock myself in a cupboard.

When I was eleven my mother realized that my theatrical streak wasn't going to go away, and that I should be encouraged to do more than pose in front of mirrors. I auditioned to become a day pupil at the Arts Educational School at the Barbican and there I felt I was in my proper element at last. As well as academic work we studied singing (at which I was very bad; I used to stand in the back of the class and mouth the words), a musical instrument (I played the guitar), drama and dance.

For dance we studied tap, modern, jazz and ballet, and though I loved all of them I decided quite early on that it was important to concentrate on just one. I wanted to be really successful at something, so I settled on ballet and from that moment I was determined to get into The Royal Ballet School.

White Lodge had a huge and glamorous reputation and we viewed it with great awe at Arts Educational. But I think what held greatest allure for me was The Royal Ballet School Book, which I had my own copy of and which I knew by heart. It was filled with pictures of the pupils in their uniforms and they looked unbelievably sophisticated to me.

Of course we had a uniform at stage school but it was less strict. At The Royal Ballet School every girl seemed to have her hair done exactly the same way and in the class photos they all wore expressions of exalted determination. I loved the pictures of the studios too, as the walls were filled with portraits of great dancers staring down at the pupils.

The Book also explained everything you needed to know about taking the audition and what they were looking for. Initially, my mother didn't think it was a good idea for me to audition; she didn't think I was disciplined enough for ballet and suspected that I was just in love with the Book. But when I was twelve I discovered that they didn't take anyone over the age of thirteen. It was my last chance to audition and I begged her to let me do it.

She finally agreed and I began to practise like mad, but I had very little idea what I should be doing. I knew that the examiners would test my hamstrings to see how loose I was so for a month I worked and worked until I could bend over and rest my head on my knees. I was so naïve. I thought, 'That's it. I can get my head on my knees, they're sure to let me in.' Did I know then that only eight places were available for the whole school that year?

The audition was spread out over three days – one of which was held at White Lodge, which is the Lower School's base in Richmond Park. It is a beautiful building, very gracious and imposing and set in lovely grounds but all I can remember is my mother sitting in a room with all the other mothers while we rushed in and out of various tests and classes.

Even at the time I realized how far behind everyone else I was because during the classes I kept doing exercises in the wrong direction and getting the steps wrong. All the other entrants looked as though they had been taking ballet exams since they were very young whereas my own training, even at stage school, had been far less formal. I'd only taken two ballet classes a week there, and I'd never had to enter an exam in my life. But I convinced myself that if I looked as if I knew what I was doing the examiners wouldn't notice. I was so confident. My mother had always instilled in me this certainty that I could do anything I wanted and it must have carried me through. Amazingly, I kept being called back after each stage of the audition and finally I was accepted. I might not have been able to perform the steps accurately but the examiners thought that I had the right physique and possibly a lot of potential.

After we'd been called into the office and the examining panel had told us that I'd been offered a place, I was naturally ecstatic. But during the months that followed, the school must often have wondered if they'd made the right decision. Because I certainly did.

My first year was terrible, and I spent most of it feeling wretched and a failure. Some of the misery was simply what any child feels when he or she goes to boarding-school for the first time and doesn't like it. I'd never wanted to go away to school as I loved my life at home, I was very close to my family and had a group of friends who I'd kept up with from primary school. But although I could have taken a day place at White Lodge I felt that I had to be a boarder because that seemed to me part of the package of a serious dance training. I wanted to do everything by the Book.

So every Sunday for months, my mother and I would go through the misery of driving me back to school after my precious weekends at home. We'd take the dogs for a walk in the park and then we'd say goodbye. I was crying and she was crying (though we didn't let each other see) and the dogs would be howling in the car. I was already feeling homesick but I was also dreading getting back into the school because I had no real friends.

I was the only new girl in my class at White Lodge, and when I arrived it was the middle of the school year and the other girls were all teamed up as best friends. Because there was an even number in the class they'd divided themselves neatly into pairs, and they seemed very upset that my arrival had spoilt the numbers. No group of people can be more spiteful than girls who want to make you feel excluded. After a few weeks I'd actually managed to make friends with the girl who had the bed next to me in the dormitory, but she decided that she wanted to be friends with someone else so when I came back to school one Sunday I found the girls had moved all my things – my duvet, my clothes and everything – to the other end of the room. They stood in a line whispering while I just stood there, shocked and humiliated.

Those early teen years are difficult for all girls as they undergo so many intense emotional and physical changes – within the same year some girls may almost be adults, while some are children still. Boarding-school exaggerates these bewildering differences because everyone is living so close together, and of course being at ballet school we were made more physically self-conscious because we were wearing leotards every day. So it was often quite a charged and difficult atmosphere.

It's hard to remember what made some girls popular and not others; in our year it was probably something as trivial as the way we did our hair. It didn't necessarily help to be good at dancing – in fact girls were usually given a hard time if they were considered to be a teacher's pet. But that of course was never a problem for me because I was so far behind the others, most of whom had been at White Lodge since they were eleven. During every ballet class I used to stand at the back of the studio and try my hardest to copy the others while I worked out what I was meant to be doing. But I was all over the place. The older pupils actually used to come and watch me through a window so that they could laugh. Even more humiliatingly, I had to go to the physio department to do special exercises because my joints had become very loose from all the gymnastics I'd done at primary school so that I didn't have enough control over my muscles. Usually pupils only went to physio if they were injured so I'd feel completely shamed when people asked what was wrong with me and I had to say, 'It's nothing.' It was just me and my body that were wrong.

At the school performance that year my class had to do the Garland Dance from Act I of *The Sleeping Beauty* and I was firmly put in the back row. I can still hear my teacher saying, 'No, Darcey, don't stand there. Go right to the back.' There was one rehearsal of that dance, though, when I was grateful for having been put in such an inconspicuous position, which was when Ninette de Valois suddenly walked in and started coaching us. Madam – who'd founded The Royal Ballet School and the company in the 1930s – was legendary. By then she was in her eighties and she didn't come into White Lodge much, but whenever she did we were all terrified. If she walked through a studio where we were being taught we wouldn't breathe for at least three minutes in case she noticed us.

When she came into the rehearsal for the Garland Dance no one was expecting her. I imagined that she'd just sit in her chair and watch, as she looked quite frail. But she was incredibly forceful. She kept trying to get up from her chair to make corrections and she was banging her stick, shouting, 'No, no, it's not meant to be like that.' I couldn't believe that so much power could come out of such a tiny woman.

So I was relieved to be in the back row then, but otherwise my position reflected very badly on my progress at the school, and when it came to my first exam I think I knew how doomed I was. Even though I tried hard to copy the girl who was in the studio with me I scraped through with almost the lowest possible mark – Pass Plus.

But at least I could hardly sink any lower, and after my teacher had bawled me out I decided I had to improve. From that point on I resolved to dedicate myself to dance and I became a bunhead.

Bunheads are like nuns, they are girls who give up everything for ballet, and in my second year I worked out a strict regime which I followed religiously. Every morning I would get up very early and go jogging round the garden to improve my stamina, copying some of the older pupils who I admired. Then every evening after supper I'd go to the studio with another girl and we'd practise all our exercises together. I also kept a wobblyboard by my bed which I used to strengthen my feet and ankles at night time, and before class I'd sit for ages with my feet jammed into the supports of the barre so that my legs were stretched as far out to the side as possible.

All of this was on top of a timetable which was already rigorous. On a weekday we'd get up at 7.30 and before breakfast we'd run to save a place at the barre with our shoebags. We were very fanatical about getting onto the top barre which had the mirror running down one side of it. The first ballet class would run from 9.00 till 10.30 or even 11.00, then we'd have a normal school day until about 3.30. After that we'd have another dance class, which might be *pas de deux*, character or Scottish, then we'd have prep for an hour or two, followed by dinner, and free time, during which we could either go and watch TV or go back and do more practice in the studio. I was the bunhead who was always in the studio. I'd abandoned my other interests.

I was a bit of an oddity in my class as no one else was so committed to their work. I remember when I first entered White Lodge I was told that my year was considered stronger in academic subjects than in dance so I would hear odd remarks like 'there she goes again' as I disappeared off to the studio every evening. But there was another girl, Jessica, who also used to practise exercises with me and by that time I didn't care what other people thought – I was in love with my new vocation. I was also very inspired by a new teacher called Patricia Linton who liked my work and, more importantly, gave us classes where I began for the first time to feel that I was *dancing* rather than just doing exercises.

During this year we also started to go on monthly trips to Covent Garden and here at last I began to understand where all my efforts were heading. Up until then I viewed dance as a physical challenge rather than as a theatrical art. But when I saw, up on the stage, all the steps which I'd been practising in class, I realized how beautiful and expressive ballet could be. I was also besotted with the costumes, the music, the lights and of course the dancers. I loved getting to know who the principals were, and spotting them in different ballets.

Strangely though I didn't have a particular star who I aspired to emulate, I didn't have a role model. When I first saw a picture of Natalia Makarova I thought the lines of her body were utterly beautiful and that the positions she held were amazing but then I was disillusioned when I discovered that she was so short. Even at school I was tall, and in those days there weren't many tall ballerinas around who I could identify with. So I tended to pick out individual qualities that I admired from different dancers – one ballerina's jump, another's legs, another's face – and piece them together into an imaginary ideal.

One older ballerina to whom I did look up was Svetlana Beriosova, who had danced with The Royal during the 1950s and early '60s. She'd been a lovely ballerina, tall and elegant with a very open quality, and she'd been my mother's favourite dancer too when she was a girl. I owned a video which included a short film of Beriosova dancing and what I loved about her was that she looked like one of us, she didn't look like a dancer from the past. Of course I also identified with her height.

While I was still a pupil at White Lodge I discovered that Beriosova taught class at Dance Works in London, and was offering private coaching, so during my summer holidays I signed up for some sessions with her. Looking back I realize how brave, or else how naïve I must have been to do them. I was only about fourteen or fifteen and I'd never been taught solos from real ballets before – maybe once a year at the School we were allowed to put a tutu on as a treat – but Svetlana immediately started trying to teach me a solo from Fokine's *Les Sylphides*. The steps in this ballet are very delicate and lyrical and there are moments of exquisite stillness as the Sylph listens for the voice of the Poet. It was completely unlike the classroom exercises I was used to and I had no idea what I was doing. I kept stopping and looking at her in awe. She was so beautiful, tall and slim with a long neck and oval face, and demonstrating the steps from *Sylphides* she had this lovely way of leaning into the air and listening. I'd try and copy her but I was very self-conscious and she'd get very strict with me and say, 'Darcey, what do you think you are doing? What are you listening for? You have to know.'

I didn't know at all but I still got terribly excited. I thought, 'This is how it's meant to be, this is real ballet dancing.' And that inspiration from Svetlana came right after a period at school when I'd at last begun to gain more confidence. I made some friends and when I passed my exam with high marks I began to feel a lot more sure of my dancing. During my last year at White Lodge I also had the extra spur of a teacher who really taught me how to push my body through space as I danced. She was called Mrs Kilgor and although she was tiny she had a huge and beautiful jump which I was enthralled by. I'd always loved jumping, it was what I could do best, and when Mrs Kilgor set us her jumping *enchaînements* I felt that I was really performing. She also made me feel happy about being tall and strong, and even a bit wild. She actually criticized the pupils who never fell over because it meant they were being too safe and conservative. I discovered how powerful and passionate dancing could be.

Jumping was the high point of my whole day. During any ballet class dancers spend a lot of time on one spot, first warming up at the barre, then in the centre of the room practising slow adages, or balances. These sections of the class always used to make me feel very constricted. Despite my hard-won self-discipline I was still restless and I always found it difficult to restrain myself. People called me Duracell because I couldn't stop moving about! But when we got to the jumping sections of class, I not only released all this pent-up energy, I also experienced a special feeling of being whole. I became my own person at last, and I could show the teachers all that I was capable of.

By the last year at Lower School, when I was sixteen, I also began to have fun. I became very close to two girls, Rachel and Alison. Alison was very funny but also extraordinarily kind; she got the nickname Mother, because she was always so sweet to everyone. I also started to stay over at weekends because there were film nights and discos for the older pupils, during which the girls were permitted very carefully controlled encounters with boys. We were allowed to dance with each other but we had to keep at least a foot apart and we absolutely couldn't touch. When I was thirteen I went out with a boy from the school called Billy Trevitt. He's now a principal with the company and as a kid he had the same rather cool and mysterious aura that he has now. But after Billy I renounced boys for ballet and it was only at the end of my last year at White Lodge that I got interested again. Actually interested is too strong a word – it was more a kind of group desperation. In the dormitory we'd be endlessly speculating about who was going out with who. And at the end of year party every girl was dying to be kissed by a boy, any boy, it didn't much matter who. I kissed Luke Heydon, who's also now a dancer with The Royal and who even now says to me, 'Don't think I don't know exactly why you kissed me at that party.'

White Lodge was a small, protected world but towards the end of our final year we began to feel very tense about who was going to be accepted into the Upper School at Baron's Court. That seemed like another planet to us, alien and remote. I'd been taken there once to perform a piece of choreography which one of my friends, Michael Rolnick, had made for me, and I had been terrified just setting foot into the building. Everyone seemed so grown up and I could even see some of the adult company members walking around. When some of the older girls came up and complimented me after I'd performed the work I could barely speak I was so in awe.

As it turned out, quite a few in my year were not accepted into the Upper School and this traumatized everyone, even those who had got a place. To me it seemed outrageously unfair that I'd been accepted while some of those who'd been at White Lodge for five years had been refused. It was my first real taste of blood, my first understanding that those of us who succeeded did so because other people had failed.

Competition is, without doubt, very brutal in the ballet world, yet I don't see any way around it. It's necessary to put even young children under pressure, not only because they need to know how to survive company life as adults, but also because they need to develop the courage and determination to go out auditioning for jobs. The teachers' constant criticism may seem like bullying but you can only make good dancers by pushing them to their limits. If only you could prevent them from getting hurt too.

When I started at Baron's Court at sixteen and a half, life felt very different. We were much less protected than at White Lodge. I went back to live at home, which was less disciplined than school of course, while a lot of the pupils went to live in digs. We'd often go back to their rooms for coffee and biscuits between classes. To me, still under the regime of family meals, it seemed incredibly liberated for someone to go out and buy a whole packet of biscuits just for themselves.

But we certainly weren't treated as adults yet and one of the worst memories of my first year was being asked to demonstrate for a guest teacher, who humiliated me thoroughly in front of an invited audience. She was giving some kind of master class and she became fixated with getting me to use my foot a certain way. I simply couldn't understand what she was instructing me to do. Everything I attempted was wrong and she kept shouting at me so impatiently that I lost my nerve and started weeping. Unexpectedly though the situation was saved for me by my heroine, Gelsey Kirkland, who happened to be in the audience.

Gelsey was a ballerina whom I'd come to admire passionately. She had danced with the two big American companies, New York City Ballet and American Ballet Theatre, and had also guested a few times with The Royal. She was tiny with an exquisitely lyrical technique but she made a huge dramatic impact on stage. At the time she was coaching at the Upper School and, having come to watch this class, she was horrified by how I was being treated. She charged into the situation like a white knight, standing up and declaring to the teacher: 'I don't blame Darcey for crying because actually I have no idea what you are trying to make her do either.'

She wrote me a letter afterwards which I still keep, in which she said:

'Like you I have cried many times in the studio, frustrated with the steps and with my teachers. You remind me that what we do when we dance is turn our tears and laughter into something truly beautiful and rare, something that makes our effort worthwhile.

Ballet technique may seem a terribly complicated way of expressing ourselves. It is difficult to explain with words . . . We must have the courage to keep asking questions. I have been dancing for more than twenty years and I am still learning, still weeping, still asking people to help me understand . . . If you should ever need me for any reason, please don't be afraid to approach me . . . Someday I am sure you will bring tears of joy to the eyes of those who watch you perform.

Sincerely, Gelsey'

That incident in the master class was typical of my progress at Baron's Court. There were some teachers who supported me, like Mrs Kilgor (who luckily continued to teach me), but others who were less convinced by my dancing as they felt I didn't suit the English style. By this point I was taller than most of the other girls in my year and however delicately I tried to dance I wasn't naturally refined and petite. So when I was sent to represent the School at the *Prix de Lausanne* I wasn't exactly every teacher's first choice.

The *Prix de Lausanne* is an international competition for young dancers which is held every year in Switzerland. It has become very prestigious, so naturally it means a lot to represent your school there, but initially the two girls chosen from The Royal were an Australian and a girl from New Zealand. This upset some people who felt that at least one English pupil should go, so I was finally selected as a compromise.

Consequently I had to go off to Switzerland knowing that some of the staff had been very unhappy about me entering, and I might have felt even more uncertain about going if I'd realized how gruelling the competition would be.

Each entrant for *Lausanne* had to prepare two solos, one classical and one modern, and the classical solo my teacher chose for me was from Act III of *Sleeping Beauty*, which didn't suit me at all. The choreography was full of hops on point, which have never been my favourite step, and when I tried to do these wearing a tutu I looked ridiculously long and gangly. So I had to be found a long dress from the school wardrobe which would cover up my legs.

My modern solo was much better suited to me, as it had been specially choreographed by one of our teachers, Diane Grey. She was a very tough, charismatic woman and I felt very charged up by her movement. I think it must have been this solo which finally won me my prize in Lausanne, although I was rather worried about her decision to use my voice for music. She made a tape of me reciting a poem about being a dancer which was then played back as I performed. I didn't refuse but I was thinking, 'But it's going to be in Lausanne, hardly anyone will be able to understand what I'm saying.'

When we finally got to Lausanne we found that everyone

was staying in the same hotel and the three of us from London found it somewhat unnerving to be eating breakfast with our school director, Merle Park. As pupils we were very intimidated by her. The first day all the entrants took class together, and we could hardly breathe, the air was so thick with tension and bitchiness. All the entrants were being sized up by each other as well as by the teachers, and those of us who came from the bigger schools like The Royal seemed to be under even more ruthless scrutiny than everyone else. After each round of the competition huge numbers of people just kept disappearing, and the class numbers got smaller and smaller. It was creepy. I remember the awful uncertainty every morning as we waited to find out if we were still in.

I was conscious that a lot of the other entrants were more assertive than I was, but I had been very carefully coached in my solos and I managed to get through them. My only serious upset occurred when I had to perform a contemporary solo which all the entrants had been given to learn during the competition. Eight bars had been choreographed for us, then we'd been left eight bars in the middle to choreograph ourselves before we went into the last section. I was a slow learner then and when I came to perform the solo I couldn't remember how to get from the section I'd choreographed into the last eight bars. I panicked and ran off stage. But there were cameras filming the whole competition, possibly for a documentary, and as I rushed towards my teacher in the wings I realized she was mouthing desperately at me, 'Darcey, you're OK. Don't cry. *There's a camera behind you.*' I looked round and saw it, and I remember just wailing in despair at how awful it all seemed. I didn't want to be there at all. But then we heard a voice over the sound system saying, 'Darcey Bussell will be able to do her piece again at the end' and my teacher became very brisk with me and said, 'There, there, you can't be *that* bad, they're giving you another chance.'

I hated taking part in the competition but I did emerge from it feeling much tougher. In the final round I had been awarded one of the three prizes given to entrants showing the most promise, and that obviously gave me a lot of confidence. Just as importantly, the competition had allowed me to compare myself with other dancers my age from around the world and I realized that I measured up.

I used the prize money to attend a summer school in Monte Carlo and that was a boost too as I not only took the students' class in the morning but also took company class with the Monte Carlo Ballet during the afternoon. I was thrilled that I could keep up with most of the adult dancers, despite being only seventeen. However, this wasn't the biggest thrill of the summer. The real excitement, which I couldn't wait to tell everyone back home, was the fact that Rudolf Nureyev was also taking class with me, in the same room.

I'd grown up thinking of Nureyev as a legend, one of the greatest stars of ballet and I was totally, totally fascinated to see him in the flesh. He came into the studio every day wearing his clogs and he didn't take them off even when he started warming up. He also dressed in an extraordinary fashion, with about three different pairs of leg warmers, layers of tee shirts and a scarf. The whole ensemble was a work of art and throughout class we'd all watch enthralled as he progressively discarded one bit of clothing after another.

The studio window was also jammed with people trying to stare at him, yet Nureyev seemed totally oblivious to us all, as though he were in a different world. His face was still very beautiful and he was extremely strong, but he seemed very old to me. He was forty-eight and obviously a long way past his physical prime. His feet were very knobbly and it was agony to watch him straining to get his leg up onto the barre. I was looking at the ruins of a great technique. He had to miss out parts of the class – I don't think he did the jumps.

The other momentous event in my first year at Upper School was being picked by Kenneth MacMillan to dance a solo in his ballet *Concerto* for the school performance. Every pupil is desperate to get a solo role in the end of year show because it's a way of getting noticed – it's a mark chalked up in your favour as you struggle towards getting into the company. So of course I was thrilled. Yet at that age, auditioning felt such a traumatic process that part of me wished I wasn't in the running for any role at all.

There were four of us being tried out for this solo, which comes in the third movement of the ballet, and all the time that we were attempting to do the steps we were also acutely aware of being looked at and whispered about. Kenneth seemed a most alarming figure. He was a big man and he sat slumped in his chair with his face showing no emotion at all. We had no idea what he was thinking but occasionally he'd whisper something to one of the staff and we would madly try to lipread – 'What's he saying, what's he saying? I'm sure he said your name.'

The audition was actually more terrifying than the show – despite the fact that the performance was the first time I'd danced on my own on the Opera House stage. I have little memory of the show except that I did the whole solo with a fixed grin on my face. It was partly nerves but also relief, because we'd rehearsed and rehearsed this ballet for so many weeks that we were just bursting to get out there and do it.

The school show is a proper public performance for members of the public as well as family and friends, and also most of the ballet critics. It was the first time I'd been judged as a professional – and fortunately I was given some encouraging reviews. Most of the critics singled me out as a promising dancer with John Percival in *The Times* describing me 'bursting impetuously through the solos of the third movement,' and Mary Clarke in *The Dancing Times* writing that I 'soared through the third movement as if it was the easiest task in the world'.

But dancers are neurotically unsure of themselves and, either by nature or by training, we only half-believe the good things that are said about us. Objectively, by the end of my first year I ought to have felt very confident about my progress, and there *were* times, in class, when I let myself think, 'Oh yes, I can do this step better than the others.' I knew that I was good. Yet I only felt that I was doing well because I worked so hard at my dancing, and it only took one critical teacher for me to think that I was the worst.

I certainly don't remember being treated as someone very

special, nor being resented by other pupils – except once when I was chosen at the end of my second (and final) year to dance in the Black Swan *pas de deux* from Act III of *Swan Lake* for the school show. There was an Australian girl who was technically a very strong dancer; she could do everything including the notorious thirty-two *fouetté* turns that come at the end of the *pas de deux* and she was furious that I'd been chosen instead of her. Typically my instant reaction to her anger was to doubt myself – I knew she was better at *fouettés* than I was and began to wonder why I'd been chosen instead of her.

Of course by the time I performed the show, the *fouettés* had been drilled into me perfectly but even so, when I reached the end of my schooling in 1987, I was as nervous as anyone else about whether I'd be taken into one of the two Royal companies. At school this was everyone's goal. Most of us at Baron's Court knew very little about the wider dance world and we didn't really consider the option of joining other companies. So acceptance into either the resident company The Royal Ballet or the touring company Sadler's Wells Royal Ballet (as it was then called) seemed like the measure of absolute success or failure.

In fact only a few students are taken each year by either company; the rest have to audition for jobs elsewhere. It turned out that I was one of only four girls in my year to be accepted. I was delighted, of course, but I wasn't exactly ecstatic, as I hadn't got the job I'd been praying for. For all of us had been accepted into what we all thought of as the much less glamorous of the two companies – Sadler's Wells.

This confused and disheartened me because as a student I had done several walk-on parts with The Royal. I remember having been thrilled when Rachel Whitebread and I were chosen to be ladies-in-waiting in *Swan Lake* because we had actually had our own costumes made for us, with our names sewn into them. We'd felt, even as students, that we were part of The Royal, and I'd believed that if I were ever to be taken into either of the companies it would be the one I'd already performed with.

But I *had* had one disastrous experience with The Royal on stage. I was acting one of the court ladies during a performance of *Sleeping Beauty* and Anthony Dowell – The Royal Ballet's director – was performing Carabosse (although Carabosse is a female character she is frequently danced by a man). At the end of the Prologue, when Carabosse is defeated by the Lilac Fairy, we all had to point at her as she drove off stage and as Anthony went past me I smiled. To me, this smile was highly expressive of the contempt I was feeling for Carabosse and my pleasure at her defeat. But when Anthony saw it he glared furiously and mouthed at me, 'What are you smiling at!'

I was petrified. When we came off stage I was gabbling to everyone else, 'ohmygod, ohmygod, what have I done! I'm going to be yelled at by *the director of the Company!*' In fact it was the rehearsal mistress who came over to discipline me, and I quickly realized that she and Anthony thought I'd been mucking around at a crucial stage in the ballet. When I explained very seriously that I'd been *acting* she sort of swallowed her words and said, 'Oh I see. Well, in any case that's wrong. Anthony doesn't *want* you to smile at him.'

So later, when I found out that I'd been taken into Sadler's and not The Royal, I immediately thought I must have a black mark against me. But I was then given the news that I would hopefully only be in Sadler's for a couple of years before transferring to The Royal and that the reason I was being sent there first was to get some experience dancing solo roles. This would not have been possible in The Royal where, in accordance with the company hierarchy, dancers have to perform several apprentice years in the *corps de ballet* before they're allowed to do solo work. In Sadler's, where there are fewer dancers and fewer rules, I'd be able to attempt solos almost immediately.

Of course that made me feel special – as if I was being put onto a fast track and had a career that the management were interested in – but my confidence dipped right down again when I started at Sadler's and one of the principals said, 'Oh that's what they told me when I first joined. And I'm still here.'

Actually she smiled as she said it, and I soon realized why she looked so cheerful because I ended up having a magical year with Sadler's. It was one of my happiest times. The company were very open and warm, they worked incredibly seriously and partied just as hard. We were away on tour a lot (The Royal Ballet gives most of the London per- formances) and the atmosphere was like a huge travelling family. Of course there were cliques and bad feelings and I had to learn about company politics – who to be wary of and who wasn't speaking to whom – but when we were performing out of London we'd all go out together every night to eat and there'd be a lot of parties.

The work was a shock at first because at school I was used to practising every role over and over again until I was perfect, while at Sadler's I was suddenly having to learn all the productions at once. I wasn't a quick learner and I remember staying up till four o'clock in the morning trying to get myself step perfect for one of my first parts in the *corps de ballet*. When it came to the show I was still petrified even though I was in the back row.

Sometimes the work was frustrating too. When Michael Corder was making his ballet *Gloriana* for the company I had what was basically a walk-on part. All I had to do was walk around with no point shoes on, wearing a mask and holding a candle. We went over and over the ballet for four weeks and all I could think was, 'Did I work so hard all those years for this?' I was desperate to get out on stage and prove myself. But otherwise the time passed in a complete whirl, as I learned one show after another.

I enjoyed being in the *corps*, even though at school I'd been hopeless dancing in a group. I was tall so I couldn't adapt easily to the other girls' steps and I kept getting out of line. My teacher would keep yelling at me, 'Watch the others, Darcey,' and then when I obeyed her she'd yell, 'But don't make it so obvious.' But at Sadler's they often put the tall women in the front row of the *corps* so everyone had to follow *me* for a change. You feel safe in the *corps* and you learn so much about being on stage and about different productions. You can watch the soloists and principals from very close up and learn how each one approaches the technical challenge of their role and how they interpret it. You start to see what style of acting works and what looks fake, you start to understand how performers control an audience. I was in complete awe of their skills, and thought I could never do anything like it.

However, after a couple of months I started to get my first solo roles. My very first was the Lilac Fairy in *Sleeping Beauty* and I doubt that I've ever been so terrified in my life. I was shaking so much that I couldn't even feel the floor with my feet. Being alone and scared on stage is a horrible feeling. It's as if you've been marooned in no man's land and you can't escape until you've finished the steps. You're desperate for the solo to end but at the same time you don't want it to be over before you've done at least one thing right.

Fortunately, at Sadler's we did so many shows that I got over my nerves quite rapidly. (The company's busy schedule also prevented me from being resented too much by the other dancers. Since most of the company had as much work as they wanted, only a few dancers felt put out by the fact that I was given solos so early on in my career.) I had the good fortune too of being looked after by the company's director, Peter Wright. He wasn't exactly a father figure but he was extremely encouraging; he always watched our performances from the wings and after a show he would always take time to go over any corrections with us. Although he wasn't intimidating I wanted to do my best for him and he always gave me new ideas about the roles I danced.

My second big solo was Queen of the Wilis in Act II of *Giselle* and I couldn't believe how little time I was given to rehearse it. When it came to my first performance I hadn't been taught the mime at all – which is very elaborate in this ballet. Luckily I was alternating the role with another dancer, Jane Billson, who was often teamed up with me. We were both unusually tall, strong dancers and we'd frequently be cast to dance the two Big Swan solos together in *Swan Lake*. On the first night of *Giselle* I was dancing in the front row of the *corps* which meant that I could watch Jane and pick up as much of the mime as possible. Then when it came to my show I had Jane in the front row and she was whispering instructions to me all the way through: 'Now you are going to say "No". Go over there. Now you're going to tell him to die.'

The Queen of the Wilis is a wonderful role to perform when you're young, and particularly when you are first making the transition from *corps de ballet* to soloist. In the corps you have to adapt yourself to the group, keeping an eye on the other dancers for your placing and timing, but as a soloist you're suddenly on your own and you have to learn how to dominate the stage. What's inspiring about the Queen of the Wilis is that she is such a powerful character. As a dancer you have to act as if you're in complete command – even if you don't feel it – so it fills you with a surge of confidence and energy. I've also always loved this solo because although it's physically exhausting it's full of jumps – which are what I do best.

The other big leap for me was earning my own money at

last. Although dancers in the *corps* earn tiny salaries (even today their take-home pay is only about £800 per month) I felt rich and independent – in fact the only time I ever felt less than totally lucky was when I met up with my non-dancing friends who were now going off to university. They appeared to have so much freedom and so much fun that my own world shrank in comparison. I couldn't party all night and sleep late with a hangover like them, or go off backpacking. Later on though, when they finished their degrees, our positions were reversed. They envied the fact that I was established in a career and had a flat of my own while they were still wondering what to do.

By the end of my first year I felt as if I'd clambered up a steep learning curve. I'd been inspired by all the challenges, I'd had a lot of fun, and I was looking forward to spending the next year or two with the company. So it came as a major shock to me when I was suddenly told that I was to leave Sadler's and join The Royal. The news came right out of the blue. I was called into Peter Wright's office and he said, 'Kenneth wants you for his new ballet, and you're going to have to join The Royal.'

Kenneth had been visiting the company recently to watch rehearsals and we all thought he must be preparing to mount one of his ballets on us. I had no idea that he'd come in to watch *me*. Peter's announcement left me floundering between two overwhelming and totally contradictory feelings: on the one hand it meant that I was about to be torn away from a company which I now regarded as family, on the other hand it meant I was about to have the most amazingly privileged opportunity. Not only was I going to join The Royal earlier than planned, but I'd been picked to dance the lead in a new MacMillan ballet. It was unheard-of. I didn't know what to say to Peter and I still hadn't taken in the situation when later that day I had to pose outside Sadler's Wells Theatre for my first encounter with the press.

When the rest of the company heard the news they didn't make me feel any less bewildered. There was always a lot of rivalry (and not much love) between the two companies so all the Sadler's dancers were making comments like, 'Ohmygod, poor you, they're all bitches in The Royal. They're terrifying.' When they heard that I was joining The Royal as a soloist and that I would have to take class with the soloists and principals and change in the same dressing room as them they made me feel like a lamb going to slaughter. There was (and still is) a very traditional hierarchy in place at The Royal which means that dancers are supposed to progress through the company one level at a time from artist (junior *corps de ballet*) to first artist (senior *corps de ballet*) then soloist, first soloist and principal. There are only about two dozen soloists and first soloists, and a dozen principals in the whole company so when I first joined I feared that many of the older dancers would be outraged by the fact that I was entering as a soloist, aged only nineteen. No one there knew who I was, no one had seen me dance.

I felt like going into Peter Wright's office and wailing, 'Why are you doing this to me?' I knew it would be so much easier for me if I joined The Royal at a lower rank, but I also knew that was impossible because I'd been cast for a principal role. It was company rules.

So when the next season started, my heart was in my point shoes as I crept into my first class at The Royal Ballet. The women in the studio all seemed much older than me and I could feel their eyes boring into me and hear them whispering as I tried to hide at the back. Once the class started I thought I was doing OK until the teacher said, 'Darcey, would you please watch how the others are doing this. You're not in *that* company now, you're in a real classical company.'

I was enraged by this remark because I was actually terribly proud of having been in Sadler's and very protective of its reputation. I thought it was a wonderful company and I hated the fact that all the dancers at The Royal felt automatically superior to it, even though most of them had never even seen Sadler's performing.

To me, the dancers at The Royal seemed much more superficial and much less committed to their work than those at Sadler's. They treated it like a day job, while in the touring company dance is a way of life. When I met up with some of my old friends from the School I was shocked by how distant I felt from them. I'd just spent a year touring and seeing the world while they had been stuck in London. I had also danced some important solo roles while they were still in the *corps* (even though people at The Royal didn't think that solo roles at Sadler's counted). So I felt I'd grown up much faster than they had. At the same time, I also felt much younger than all the other soloists, and it felt very awkward when I had to share a dressing room with six of them at the Opera House.

I tried to ease the situation by being very deferential and asking them lots of questions. I knew they must resent me being there because of course I was going to be dancing some of their roles, and I knew that if I behaved too confidently I would be disliked. After a while they saw that I was working hard and that I wasn't behaving like a pushy upstart so they accepted my presence. A few of the older dancers were also quite protective of me, particularly Lesley Collier. But even so I felt very alienated for a long time, as if I didn't belong anywhere in the company at all.

It didn't help either that The Royal was so much bigger a company so it took me a long time to get to know who everyone was. At Sadler's we were all thrown together: I got to know the director, Peter Wright, and most of the principals, because we'd all go out to eat in the same restaurant after a show or we'd all be performing in the same tent somewhere in Cambridge on tour. At The Royal I didn't speak to the director, Anthony Dowell, for months. I barely encountered him and when I did I felt so awed by him I'd never dare to talk. He had been such a star in the ballet world, I'd grown up through school knowing that he was The Royal's greatest male dancer. I remember my shock the first time I performed the Lilac Fairy and he was Carabosse – and he actually gave me a wink! Quite a change from my reprimand for smiling a couple of years earlier!

The other challenge which made my first few months at The Royal so nerve-racking was that I had to learn a whole new repertoire of ballets. Even though the two companies perform many of the same ballets, their productions are very different. So the work itself felt as daunting to me as if I'd just come out of school.

Luckily the most terrifying prospect, dancing the lead in Kenneth MacMillan's new ballet, was postponed. Kenneth had been very ill for a few months so although we began work on *The Prince of the Pagodas* soon after I joined The Royal, we took rehearsals slowly. The delay at least gave me a chance to settle into my new life and to perform some solo roles with the company before I took on my first three-act ballet. I created a role in David Bintley's new one-act ballet *Spirit of Fugue* (though Kenneth was rather cross about it and I remember him arguing with someone: 'I brought her into the company to do *my* work, not David's'), and I also danced the Lilac Fairy in *Sleeping Beauty*, which was the first time I shared a stage with Sylvie Guillem.

I had mixed feelings about Sylvie, who had only recently joined the company after leaving Paris Opéra. She had a very grand manner, which had been partly instilled in her at the Opéra where the hierarchy is even more powerful than at The Royal, and senior principals are expected to behave like megastars. She also had an awesome technique which made me feel very junior (even though I was only four years younger than her). She got very cross with me during one performance of *Sleeping Beauty* because she said that I'd stood in front of her: 'They cannot see me,' she muttered to me, 'and they want to see me.' But Sylvie was a wonderful dancer to watch and learn from and of course she was tall like me, which made me feel much less conscious of my height.

For that first performance of *Beauty* I'd felt quite confident dancing the steps of the Lilac Fairy solo but I'd been scared of the mime which I hadn't had to perform in the Sadler's production. The mime sequence actually starts before the music and during the show I was too slow making my first gestures, which meant I then got into a panic trying to catch up without missing out essential points of the story. Anthony was performing Carabosse and going cross-eyed at me as he tried to cue me in: 'That's right, turn round and look at the baby.'

During my first year I was also cast to dance Gamzatti in Natalia Makarova's new production of *La Bayadère*. Natasha, who was a legendary ballerina herself, liked to wield a lot of power during rehearsal and I was very intimidated by her presence. But my real troubles with the role arose from the fact that she wanted us to perform *Bayadère* in a very Russian style. I'd always assumed that acting should feel natural, and true to my own feelings, while the kind of acting Natasha wanted seemed to me very histrionic and false. At first I couldn't do it. I'd take one step and she'd go, 'No, that's not it.' Then I'd start again and she'd shout, 'No, you're getting married, you must feel it *here*,' and bang her chest. I felt as if I would never be allowed to get going.

Of course she was perfectly right. *Bayadère* needs to be performed in a very flamboyant, colourful style and Natasha gave us some wonderful ideas for dramatizing the big climaxes, like the confrontation scene. This is where Gamzatti has to grab Nikiya by the scruff of her neck and throw her across the stage. In this production, Sylvie was dancing Nikiya and I have to admit it was terribly pleasing to be able to throw her across the stage. I felt I had her. But she was very good about it – she has a surprising sense of humour. If I was ever a bit too rough with her she'd laugh and say, 'Yes, you're strong, I gather.'

By this time I was also working on *The Prince of the Pagodas*, creating the role of Princess Rose, and that was proving to be the most daunting test ever of my nerve and my technique. I'd never performed the lead role in a three-act ballet before and I'd certainly never had one created on me, but luckily Fiona Chadwick, who was dancing my evil sister Epine, looked after me. I was fully prepared to throw myself into every step asked of me. I'd have spun around on my head if Kenneth had asked me to but Fiona taught me how to pace myself. You can't dance a three-act ballet the way you would dance a solo role or you would kill yourself.

Because we had a longer than usual rehearsal period for creating the work, Kenneth was having fun making each act harder and more complicated as we went on. Fiona and my partner Johnny Cope (who was dancing the Prince) kept warning me, 'Make sure you say it's difficult. As soon as Kenneth thinks you can do something easily, he just makes it harder for you.' Kenneth changed the choreography so often that Johnny and I often used to get confused about which version of a *pas de deux* we were meant to be dancing.

Johnny was older and much more experienced than I was

and it often seemed to me that he danced everything perfectly, while all the mistakes we made were my fault. I felt very young and insecure but I didn't want anyone to know it so I'd hold back my tears until I reached the dressing room – and then I'd weep and weep.

But I learned so much from making *Pagodas*, about how to hold the stage when you are at the centre of a ballet, about being partnered and, above all, about working with a choreographer. Kenneth would often ask us to work out solutions to moves that he'd started, so that for instance we might be stuck in some complicated position that he'd got us into, and then he'd say, 'Now, if you take his hand out from under your leg and turn, how would you finish?' We were constantly trying out new moves, and we truly felt as though we'd contributed to the ballet.

The rehearsal period went on for so many months that by the time we got to the opening night on 7 December 1989 I felt rather as I'd done before my first school performance. I just wanted to get out on stage and dance. I wasn't so much nervous as dazed and throughout the show I just went flat out for every step without being aware of the audience, or the significance of the occasion. Even after the curtains went down I still wasn't sure where I was. Then Anthony Dowell came up to me and told me that I'd been made a principal. I think that all I could manage to say was, 'Are you sure?'

2

MY DANCING DAY

BEING MADE A principal on that first night of *Pagodas* changed the course of my life dramatically. I could look forward to dancing the great classical roles of which I'd dreamt like Juliet, Giselle, Odette and Odile. I would also, later, begin to understand what it means to be a public person. But it took months for my new situation to sink in because on a day-to-day basis my routine didn't change. As dancers we go through the same schedule whether we're a member of the *corps de ballet* or a prima ballerina: class and rehearsal, five or six days a week.

My working day begins now as it did then, at 7.30 or 8.00 a.m. when I get up and eat breakfast. I always have a big bowl of cereal, a mixture of Weetabix, Alpen and Special K which lasts me for hours. If I don't have a show in the evening I'll probably do a session of body conditioning, in which a trainer works with me to tone my muscles and work on my weak spots. Then I take company class which runs from 10.30 to 11.45 and which every dancer has to do every day. Class is like brushing your teeth – if you don't do it your body starts to rot!

I like to vary which class I do, so if I'm in the mood for some energetic jumping and turns I will join the men's. But with each class we always start slowly, warming our bodies up bit by bit. If I've performed a show the night before it's usually a struggle getting started as my body feels stiff and aching. But I'm always well wrapped up, with socks over my shoes and some kind of woollen all-in-one, so that I get warm very quickly. Over the years I've learned what clothes work best for me. Dancers love to sweat. It lubricates the machinery.

In the middle of a busy season we don't usually want a demanding class, we simply need to wake up our bodies for the long day ahead and touch base with our technique. One of my favourite teachers is Betty Anderton who's wonderful at getting us on our legs in the morning. She knows the company well, and though she works on our weak points she also accepts that if we have a hard week we need to pace ourselves. Sometimes we get guest teachers coming into the company who tend to be very enthusiastic about pushing our technique. They want to challenge us and show off their teaching skills, which is exciting for us if we're in the middle of a slack period but we don't have time for that level of concentration if we have a very busy schedule.

The less experienced dancers in the company are very dependent on teachers for corrections and encouragement so they are rightly given the most attention during class. Principals obviously need corrections too – our teachers are crucial to us all our working lives – but we can also take more responsibility for ourselves, and I now know my body well enough to understand what I have to concentrate on. My upper back is much stiffer than my lower back so I have to work on loosening it up, and I have to be very careful with my right ankle where I've suffered a serious stress injury in the past.

I use the mirror in the studio all the time because it shows up most of the faults that need correcting. Dancers have a reputation for being vain or self-obsessed because we look at ourselves in mirrors the whole time, but the way we look is completely different from someone who is trying on clothes in a shop. While we're working, we're not so much looking at ourselves as at the line and action of our bodies. It's as if we are seeing ourselves in the abstract. In lots of ways the mirror is very unforgiving – every day it insists on showing every flaw in our bodies and our techniques – but I also think of it as a friend. If we're on tour and working in strange studios and theatres, the mirror is always a way to get hold of ourselves and help us find our centre. I often find that I look at other people in the mirror too because I can often spot-check my own faults by seeing what other dancers are doing.

After class we have a fifteen-minute break, but for the women in particular this is never much of a rest. Most of us have to change our point shoes, as we tend to do class in a soft, broken-down pair and we need to put on a harder pair for rehearsal. We also plaster up our feet, putting strips of Elastoplast over our toes to protect them from getting blistered and calloused. We may even change into fresh practice clothes if we've become very hot during class. Then we have rehearsals, which may go on until about six in the evening if there isn't a show. We usually break at around 1.30 for lunch although I don't like to eat much in the middle of the day other than fruit. If I'm going to be thrown around a lot in a *pas de deux* during the afternoon, I don't like to have a full stomach or I start to feel queasy. I also like to know that I'm light for my partner.

People seem to be fascinated by what dancers eat and most of us are unusually careful about our diet. Obviously our job requires us to keep in shape so we are calorie-conscious, but we also try to eat the kinds of food that will give us the most energy. At least we do when we are older and more experienced. When I was young, I was like every-one else my age and I'd eat anything that would fill me up and keep me going, and until I was twenty-five I used to be able to eat platefuls of food without it showing on my body at all. During school I hadn't been taught anything about nutrition and it wasn't really an issue; hardly anyone had obvious weight problems and we felt that we had energy to spare. Even though there were a couple of girls who became badly anorexic the illness wasn't discussed as a potential danger to the rest of us. We were concerned about these girls, as our fellow pupils, and were angry that their problems hadn't been spotted earlier. But we didn't relate it to ourselves.

Now I'm much better informed about nutrition, and I also have to be more cautious about what I eat if I'm going to maintain my average weight, which is eight and a half stone. On ordinary work days I'll probably have a cup of tea and a muesli bar at about four o'clock in the afternoon and then eat my main meal at home, which will often be pasta with a light sauce. My diet is healthy these days and I don't usually drink alcohol during the week. But I hate to be considered fussy so I like to eat what other people are eating when we go out to restaurants or to friends, and though I've never been a good cook I do like to experiment in the kitchen.

If I'm dancing a performance in the evening then I'll eat a reasonable lunch at about four o'clock. It will usually be a bowl of pasta salad or a sandwich, followed by a lot of water, a banana or yoghurt and maybe some digestive biscuits. Then I won't eat anything else until after the show. If I've danced a three-act ballet then I'm always starving by the end and afterwards I often eat out with my husband, Angus, or some friends and family. But I'll still be feeling on such a physical high from the show that however hungry I am it's difficult to sit down and eat very much. If the show is in the middle of the week I don't stay out late anyway, and if I'm specially busy the next day I go straight home.

When I'm on holiday I do like to have at least a week or two when I'm not being diet-conscious at all. At The Royal

Ballet we have five weeks' holiday during the summer and for two of those I always try to cut off completely. It's important to be able to forget about being a dancer because that way the body is able to recover much more quickly from the strains of the season. But after a fortnight I tend to focus on work again; I start pushing my body by swimming in the sea till it hurts, and I stop eating chocolate. Christmas is hard as we don't really have a holiday like everybody else. I like to be able to eat a big dinner with the rest of my family, with mince pies and everything, but then it always feels very hard getting back to work the next day. Ballet is an unforgiving profession. The lucky ones don't have to worry much about their weight, but there are some lovely dancers who've left the stage because they've become so sick of having to fight their weight every day of their lives.

There are some periods when I'm not conscious of my weight at all, and when I have to eat more than usual because I'm working so hard. During a really hectic time I can be rehearsing up to four ballets a day as well as performing a couple of shows a week. Non-dancers are often startled by how much choreography we have to learn and how quickly we do it. Obviously when we first join a company this comes as a shock as we've only been used to having short solos or classroom exercises demonstrated to us but we are trained to pick up information, both visually and musically, and with experience we become much faster at picking up both the shape of a phrase and all its details. We can also assimilate corrections much faster.

If I'm working on a new ballet then rehearsals take up the

largest chunk of the day, because choreographing is a slow and exhaustive business and the dancers have to be in the studio most of the time. When I'm rehearsing old repertoire I don't spend much time working with other dancers until we come together for the full company calls. Most of my time is spent with my partner and my coach, Donald MacLeary, who runs me through solos and *pas de deux*.

Donald has been coaching me since I first joined the company and he's always been a crucial support. He has a wonderful eye, and is amazingly thorough so even when we go through a ballet like *Swan Lake*, which I've been dancing for nine years now, he reminds me of critical points to remember as well as suggesting new possibilities. Of course he doesn't change the choreography, but pointing out a different way of going into a step or a slightly different musical emphasis can make a dramatic difference. If I'm having difficulty with a step he can find the perfect image, or the exact correction that will transform it into the easiest thing.

These classic roles are so huge that there's always more to learn about them and Donald has as high ambitions for me as I have for myself. He builds my confidence and makes me believe that I can push myself beyond my limits. He has a wonderful repertoire of stories, having worked with some of the most famous dancers in the world including Margot Fonteyn. He had the knack of making ballerinas feel so confident when he partnered them that Natasha Makarova dragged him out of retirement, she wanted to dance with him so badly.

I'm also coached by Monica Mason, The Royal's assistant

director. She was a ballerina with the company from 1967 to 1984 so she has an impressive knowledge of the ballets we dance and of the choreographers who made them. She's particularly brilliant at explaining the point of a solo to us immediately. Sometimes we can be rehearsing a role for weeks without fully understanding the qualities we should be finding in it – whether the movement should be strong, lyrical or fragile; whether we should be focusing on the action of the feet or the arms; or what the dramatic motivation for the steps is. Monica, without fail, gives us all the right clues at the first rehearsal. At the same time she's very open to ideas from us – she doesn't, like some coaches, expect us to dance a role exactly as she sees it. She knows that we need to find ourselves within it.

Monica also gives us private coaching when we're recovering from injury, and during one of my own long periods of convalescence I got to know her very well. She's astonishingly patient and understanding. Being injured is always very bad for a dancer's morale and she knows that it's sometimes as useful for us to spend a half-hour session weeping on her shoulder as it is exercising our bodies. Even if we aren't injured but are feeling insecure about our dancing she'll give us private coaching. She analyses our technique in minute detail, even down to the way in which we flex and point our big toe, and can often pinpoint straight away some bad habit that's been hampering our dancing.

The other person who coaches me is Anthony Dowell, and though Monica and Donald each have an incredible eye Anthony's is the best. I don't think he realizes how much we treasure his appearances in rehearsal. We hang on to every word he says, and we'd love to make a tape of him speaking and play it through when he's not there.

Part of his power is obviously the fact that he's the company director, which means that we all magically dance better as soon as he's in the studio. We're so eager to show him everything we can do, and a compliment from him means more to us than any amount of applause from an audience. But we also long for him to give us personal corrections because they are always so revealing. He had such a natural dance talent himself and even now, when he demonstrates how a step should be, his dancing is breathtakingly fluid. There's never any hesitation or any fudging.

He also has a great memory for his own past performances and is very willing to trade secrets of what he used to find difficult or scary as well as what kind of tricks he used to get him through. A lot of older dancers tend to say, 'Oh darling, you won't have any problem with that, I never did,' and though they may be trying to reassure us, it really doesn't help.

Yet some of the most inspiring rehearsals I've ever had have been with older dancers who either performed in the original production of a ballet or who danced it a long time ago. They make me feel as if I'm plugged into the history of the work. The choreography comes alive because it's not just recorded in the choreologist's (or notator's) notation. It's in these dancers' memories and their bodies.

When I was rehearsing the role of the Black Queen in Ninette de Valois's *Checkmate* I had some illuminating rehearsals with Beryl Grey, who danced it during the 1940s. It was lovely being in the studio with her. Of course I'd never seen her dance but I knew so much about her and felt so honoured to have her teaching me. I was so surprised too that she turned out to be the same height as me, which is rare for a dancer of her generation. We could actually look at each other eye to eye, and I didn't feel like a giraffe. Beryl had danced some of the steps in a slightly different way from the choreography I'd been taught and I always find those differences fascinating. They make me aware of how the ballet has changed for each generation.

But the greatest revelation was being coached by Margot Fonteyn, who came into the company a few times to rehearse me for the role of Odette/Odile in *Swan Lake*. This came at the best possible time for me as I was only just twenty and I'd done only one performance of the ballet. For some reason I had been rushed into the first show, with only two weeks to learn it. So during the performance all I'd been able to focus on was getting through the steps. I hadn't had any space or time to think about the role itself.

Margot though was hardly interested in the steps, she wanted me to understand the character I was dancing, and everything she suggested was incredibly vivid and an astonishing revelation. She said that I should imagine Odette as a woman, not as a swan – which is how I'd always viewed the role. She said, 'Even though Odette has swan mannerisms it is as a woman that Siegfried is attracted to her.' Then she took me through the mime scenes and gave me reasons for everything I did, so that for the first time the story started to make emotional sense to me. There's a moment when Odette is explaining to Siegfried about the curse that's been laid on her and she gets so angry that she steps right up to him. Immediately she realizes that she's come far too close, that she's on dangerous ground, and she draws back. The only instructions I'd been given for performing this moment was that I should take two steps this way and one step that way. I hadn't been given any motive for the action at all.

Margot also taught me how to use my eyes. She had beautifully expressive eyes herself, and it's very important how the dancer uses them in the second act of *Swan Lake*. During much of this act Odette and Siegfried are alone together on stage and the ballerina needs to make her eyes speak for her, so that he and the audience can understand the intensity of her emotions.

It was magical learning all these things from Margot, and I was in a trance of combined terror and wonder. She was much sterner than I had expected, although that may have been because she was very ill by then and everything was an effort for her. She had difficulty getting in and out of her chair so she had to stand all through the rehearsal.

Yet though she was so frail she projected an aura of extraordinary grandeur and mystery. The air seemed to hover around her. She held herself beautifully, her smile was perfectly gracious and even though she was tiny compared to me, I felt very small. I'd seen hundreds of pictures of her and lots of film, but I was still amazed by her elegance and beauty.

*

Most of my working days are more routine of course, and in between rehearsals for ballets I often try to squeeze in a massage or a session with the physio department since our bodies cannot work day-in day-out without being pampered and readjusted. During the week I, like all the women in the company, also have to find space to work on my point shoes, which is an extremely time-consuming – and very personal – business.

All dancers are very picky about what kind of shoes they like to dance in and how they prepare them. They don't just wear what they are given. So at the beginning of a week we all go to the shoe department and pick out about ten pairs of shoes. We need that many to get us through a week of rehearsal and performances, especially if we are doing a three-act ballet like *Sleeping Beauty*. Dancing Aurora, I may wear out three or four pairs during a single show.

Once we've chosen the shoes we then have to customize them, which is a major chore as it takes about half an hour per pair. I always start by pouring a thin layer of shellac or glue inside the sole which sets hard and makes the shoes last longer. Then I take the sole out and blade it with a razor knife all around the edge so that it's thinned down. After that I put the inside sole back in and blade the bottom of the shoe so that it's thin and flat, allowing me to feel the floor easily through it, and scar the sole so that it has a good grip. Then I cut the satin off the toe which also gives the shoe more grip, and finally sew on two elastics and a pair of ribbons – everyone likes to have these in slightly different places to suit their own feet.

Aged nine, at Fox Primary School swimming gala
© *Darcey Bussell*

Aged thirteen: my official photograph
on entrance to White Lodge
© David Ingham

My first school performance on the Opera House stage

© *Leslie E Spatt*

My first *Swan Lake*, aged twenty
© *Leslie E Spatt*

My first *La Bayadère* solo (centre)
with Viviana Durante and Karen Paisey

© *Leslie E Spatt*

Kenneth MacMillan coaches Jonathan Cope and me
in *The Prince of the Pagodas*
© *Anthony Crickmay*

Natalia Makarova rehearses me as Gamzatti
in *La Bayadère* (aged nineteen)
© *Anthony Crickmay*

Dancing Terpsichore in *Apollo*
© *Leslie E Spatt*

After all that I have to wear them in because a brand-new point shoe is too hard and noisy to wear on stage. The ends are made out of layers of shellac and wadding – basically a kind of papier mâché – so I break them down either by wearing them in during rehearsal or by banging them hard on a stone step for about ten minutes until the ends are almost crumbling. Some principal dancers like to prepare seven or eight pairs before a show and then decide which they'll wear at the last minute, but that's too much of a choice for me. I limit myself to two pairs for a one-act and four for a three-act ballet.

A shoe can make or break a performance and I'll sometimes deliberately rehearse in a pair that are really bad just in case I end up wearing terrible shoes in a show – at least that way I'll be prepared for the worst. For a romantic ballet like *Giselle* or *Romeo and Juliet* I like my shoes to be as soft and quiet as possible so I break the papier mâché right down. A ballet like *Sleeping Beauty* involves a lot of balancing and turning so I need more support from the shoes and don't break them down quite so much. I also need to select a pair that have a good flat base on the toe as some shoes can be bit lumpy at the end. Some also have a much more flattering shape than others because of the way they're cut, so I try to put those aside for a show. Dancers are always trying out different manufacturers to find the perfect shoes.

As well as preparing our shoes we have to make time for costume fittings. When dancers are first tried out for one of the big classical roles they usually borrow someone else's costume (the first time I danced Nikiya in *La Bayadère* I borrowed Sylvie's because she has a long body like me) but once we're established in a principal role we are given our own costume for it, which is made exactly to our measurements. However, being fitted for costumes in a new production is very time-consuming; we have to stand for an hour like a tailor's dummy while the dressmakers are pinning and sewing.

Some designers are very fussy about their costumes and everything has to be made in exact accordance with their vision of the ballet. *The Prince of the Pagodas*, for example, was designed by Nicholas Georgiadis who is a legend in the theatre and had *very* definite ideas about what he wanted. Unfortunately his vision involved putting me in a boned corset, and though this looked impressive since it flattened my torso and prevented any wrinkles from appearing in the bodice, it was very hard to dance in. Boned corsets don't leave any room for my ribs to expand as I move, and since I'm quite broad anyway I feel constricted. Luckily Georgiadis let me have one elasticated panel at the back, which made all the difference.

I was so young then that I'd never have dared stand up to him, but now I've learned a lot about what will and won't make a costume look good on me – and I know that it's worth being fussy. If I'm tired during a fitting and don't bother to involve myself in the details I'll almost always end up with a costume that doesn't look perfect. If all the dresses have short skirts then I need to have mine a little bit longer than most of the other women's because otherwise my legs look ridiculously long in comparison. I also know that a skirt which ends mid-calf is unflattering to anyone's legs – it makes the calves look huge.

It is also critical to have enough time to rehearse in our costumes before opening night as some problems don't show up until we start dancing. When we performed Mikhail Baryshnikov's production of *Don Quixote* all the women were put in asymmetrical skirts, longer on one side than the other, and although they looked beautiful the uneven length put everyone slightly off centre in their pirouettes.

Another awkward costume was the one I wore for Christopher Wheeldon's ballet *Pavane pour une Infante Défunte*. It had a long wrap-around satin skirt which my partner, Johnny Cope, had to unwind as I started dancing. The first time we tried it, it ruined the effect of my entrance because as I began to *bourrée* down stage my knees could be seen knocking against the skirt. I was meant to look as if I was floating, not wobbling. We couldn't change the costume at this stage, so to create the right effect I had to dance the steps with my feet turned in, and with my legs slightly bent so that I didn't disturb the skirt. When I practised this without the skirt on I looked very bizarre. But the skirt looked good and the designer was happy.

In *Pavane* I was also wearing a boned bodice, and that caused problems too. One of the lifts became very dangerous for us to do because Johnny couldn't find my back through the bodice and couldn't get any grip. The whole *pas de deux* threatened to fall apart, but we solved it by sewing little sticky tapes all around my waist and back so that Johnny's hand didn't slip.

However much we rehearse in advance there are always going to be performances when our costumes play tricks on stage. It's very easy for a woman wearing an elaborate tutu to get hooked onto her partner's jacket during a *pas de deux* – so that they both become stuck in a ridiculous embrace, frantically trying to extricate themselves without the audience noticing. But my own worst costume disasters involved buttons and a headdress.

The buttons incident occurred during a performance of *Pagodas*, where Johnny was bringing me down from a high lift. As I descended, my costume caught on one of his buttons, and it came off with a loud pop. We started to giggle, but as he brought me down lower I caught on all the rest of them. The buttons were flying everywhere – pop . . . pop . . . pop – one after the other, and rolling all over the stage; of course we became terrified because if we stepped on one we'd have gone flying.

Then there was the Grand *Pas de Deux* in *Sleeping Beauty*, where my headdress started to come loose after a very fast succession of pirouettes. During my partner's solo (it was Stuart Cassidy) I was able to run off stage and stick in lots more hair pins but after my next entrance it started to detach itself again and during the coda (the final duet) it came right off. It was hanging off the back of my head with the string stuck in my hair and we were unable to rip it off. The coda winds up to a big climax of supported pirouettes and we couldn't think what other step to do – we had just done some big *jetés* – so I started the pirouettes, hoping for the best. Unfortunately every time I whipped round the headdress hit me in the cheek while Cassidy, behind me, was having to flinch back to avoid being slugged in the jaw – it was very heavy and sharp. At the last turn, which was very fast, he got whacked incredibly hard – and we could hear the audience going 'ooowww'.

During the week running up to the first night of a production our schedule changes because we have to get the ballet onto the stage. There may be four stage calls (rehearsals on stage) during this time, to allow different casts to experience the set and the lighting, and then the general or dress rehearsal.

Dancing on stage is a completely different sensation to dancing in a studio. It gives us such an altered sense of space that it's almost like being in another ballet. In a studio the walls contain us – our energy bounces back off them – but on stage we have no walls or ceiling and we have to project far out across the huge expanse of the auditorium. We have to create that special illusion in dance that the movement is still travelling through the air, even after we've physically stopped.

However, when I first performed on stage I didn't know how to deal with this and it was almost as if I put a blanket over my head while I danced. I was concentrating so hard on the choreography that I couldn't connect with anything beyond me. I was also scared of projecting too much with my acting; I thought I would look too exaggerated, too over the top. Then I saw a video of myself and realized how boring it looked when I performed as if I were still in a studio. The difference of scale to which we have to accommodate on stage is unbelievable.

We need our stage calls to get used to the lighting as well as the space, because that too can be a shock. Audiences don't realize that when dancers are on stage they are frequently looking into pitch darkness or else being dazzled by lights – and it's often unpredictable which it will be. I remember once dancing Act II of *Swan Lake* and finding that I had taken a step forward into what became total blackness. For a few seconds I didn't know which direction I was facing, or even where the orchestra was.

There's a moment in Act II of *Cinderella* that's always very scary, where she has to circle around the stage twice, ending up doing dozens of little *chaîné* turns. Even in the studio this is alarming as the whole room becomes a whirling blur. It's horrible. You're just thinking, 'Please, please, I want to be able to see again.' On stage it's twice as bad, because you suddenly have lights shining right at you from every direction and they make it almost impossible to find a spot to focus on during the turns. (When a dancer 'spots' during pirouettes she fixes her eyes on a particular place and then, as she turns, whips her head around to find the spot again as quickly as possible. The spot not only works as a compass point to keep her sense of direction but prevents her from getting too dizzy.) Sometimes I spot on the first wings, where there's a dark rim, or else I keep my eyes fixed on one of the dancers on stage. This can be rather dismaying for them and I remember absolutely terrifying one dancer: I fixed my eyes on her and smiled like mad to cover up the fact that I was feeling so dizzy and as I headed towards her she thought I was going to land right on top of her – like a missile in target practice.

During the week of stage calls I always find it hard to pace myself. I want to spend as much time as possible on stage but don't want to wear myself out before the big opening. I try to cut down on rehearsals in the studios, and focus each day on running through a single act or doing my solos. But the general rehearsal is always tough. We're meant to treat it as a proper performance and since there is always an audience present, we have to dance well. The problem is that if it's a long, hard ballet then we're afraid of dancing flat out because that will leave us tired for the next day.

On the morning of a first night I try hard to kid myself that it's just a normal day so that I don't exhaust myself by getting nervous, but I don't always succeed. I take morning class as usual and then, if I'm only going to be dancing a one-act ballet, I may carry on rehearsing other productions until about 4.30 when I start to get ready for the show. If I'm performing a full-length work then I'll take the day more leisurely. I might rehearse on my own in a studio for a while, then have some lunch and head for the Green Room in the Opera House. Some dancers like Johnny Cope prefer to go home and rest, but I'm scared of switching off completely and then finding it hard to drag myself back into the theatre. In the Green Room I'll put my feet up and physically relax, trying to keep my mind as empty as possible by flipping through magazines.

Getting ready for the stage always takes a lot of time,

though some ballets are more complicated than others. I do my own make-up, which takes about half an hour unless the designer has specified something more elaborate, and our hairdresser, Juan, does my hair. He's very liberal with the hair spray and I usually end up with the whole bottle over my head. This feels horrible but at least I know my hair is secure. Then I'll do class on stage for half an hour during which I like to work by myself. Though some dancers prefer warming up together, I use the time to get mentally prepared for the show.

After warming up I go back to my dressing room to finish getting ready, and as I put on my costume I can start to feel myself transforming into character. Something magical always happens when I dance in costume for the first time, as if the ballet is taking over. Obviously this transformation feels most extreme in a work that involves putting on a very elaborate dress and wig; I always love changing into the black dress in Act II of *Manon* as it makes me feel so gorgeous. But even with a non-story ballet like *Pavane* I can get deeper into the ballet's atmosphere just by putting on the costume. The dress is very vampish, very 1940s, and its style draws me into a different world.

The effect of dancing in costume doesn't just make us *feel* the part, it makes us move differently too. Though a wig often feels odd when we put it on, it pulls the head back and alters our carriage so that we move more grandly. I like false eyelashes too because they make me more conscious of my eyes and I use them better. Even jewellery can help. Some people find it distracting but to me it finishes off the role.

The more glitter I have, the more imposing I feel. The costume affects our dancing enormously. It doesn't matter how many times we've rehearsed in the studio we always dance differently in costume whether it's because it is heavier or tighter, or because the skirt swings in a certain way.

Then, from the moment the curtain goes up, I'm busy all the time. While I'm waiting to go on I talk to myself non-stop in the wings, reminding myself to keep calm and relax my shoulders (which tend to go up when I'm excited) and reassuring myself that I won't get tired and that I've rehearsed everything well. Even while I'm dancing I'm usually giving myself corrections all the time so there's a tiny analytic part of my brain still ticking over. Only in very dramatic ballets like *Romeo and Juliet*, where the steps are so much part of the character and where the music sweeps me along, do I give in to a role completely.

There have been occasional performances, during which I've been ill or injured, when I've simply had to concentrate on getting through the steps and haven't been able to keep up this internal running commentary. Ironically, people have complimented me afterwards, saying how calm I looked! But usually I need to feel on edge to dance my best, I'm afraid of the role slipping away from me otherwise. So even when I might look as though I'm resting – after I prick my finger in *Sleeping Beauty* and am lying on the floor – I'm actually running in my head all that I have to do in the next act. I'm also listening closely to the music, because when the men come to pick me up I like to arch my back slightly to make it easy for them to get their arms under me. I always hear this little whisper, 'Thanks, Darce.'

One of the hard things about dancing – particularly in classical ballets – is that the performance doesn't just depend on us, the dancers. Conductors especially can affect us because they determine the speed of the music, and if they hear it differently from us it can throw our whole performance.

When we have a conductor like Victor Fedotov guesting from the Kirov it's a great luxury because he takes his speeds from the dancers, unlike many conductors over here who don't adjust their tempi at all – they play the music as they would a concert score. In Russia dancers seem to wield more power though, so conductors like Fedotov will speed up or slow down the orchestra to suit the dancing.

When we work with him it's wonderful to get so much attention, but it can be unnerving. At first I couldn't get used to the way he'd virtually stop the orchestra whenever I took a balance, and wait for me to come down before he started up again. Because I'm so used to having to keep time with the orchestra I kept on balancing longer and longer as he slowed down, and both the music and I nearly ground to a halt.

Since most Opera House conductors don't indulge us in the same way we have to adjust our speeds to them. It's fine if everyone's rehearsed together but if a new conductor comes in or there hasn't been enough preparation time then the music may be played at an alarmingly different speed from the way we've rehearsed it. It's a terrible feeling – you're being forced off the music and you can't do the steps properly. Dancers often come off the stage in tears because a conductor has spoilt their show. Being tall, I generally prefer conductors to take speeds slightly slow. If the music goes too fast I can't always fit in the steps and I'm in danger of tripping over myself. If it goes too slow I can always save something, I can always pull a phrase out longer – except of course when I'm jumping. I can't actually fly.

Fortunately we have recently appointed a new music director, Andrea Quinn, at The Royal, who will be conducting for us regularly. I have a close relationship with Andrea anyway as I danced for her when she was taking part in a ballet-conducting competition (Billy Trevitt and I performed *Swan Lake*). But now that she's with the company full time she is getting to know everyone and is extremely generous and attentive. She discusses speeds with all the principals during stage calls, and even in the middle of a show will come backstage for a quick chat during intervals just to double-check for the next act.

Though conductors may cause us some of our most frustrating moments on stage, audiences tend not to notice these as much as the technical mistakes we make. We can't cover up a wobble or a bad fall, and there are some notorious black spots in the repertoire, such as the Rose Adage in *Sleeping Beauty* or the thirty-two *fouettés* in *Swan Lake* which have daunted all dancers ever since they were choreographed. When we dance *them* we always know that half the audience are watching and waiting for us to slip up.

The steps which trip dancers up in the Rose Adage are the

LIFE IN DANCE

balances on point in *attitude*. These aren't difficult in the studio – any principal dancer should be able to do them easily – but they occur very early on in the role when the ballerina hasn't had time to feel her way into the show, and they are performed in the middle of the stage so that she feels terribly exposed. All the other dancers are staring at her as well as the audience.

She also has other things to worry about besides managing to hold a balance on one leg, the first of which is that she has to pull the balance off not once but eight times (four balances in one section of the Adage, four in another). At this point in the ballet Aurora is being courted by a quartet of princes and each one in turn has to take her hand, hold her steady, then let go as she takes her balance. So with each man the ballerina is having to adjust to a different grip. One man's hand may be a bit shaky while another may hold so tightly that it's difficult to let go. It's much harder than being partnered by a wooden barre.

At the same time Aurora has to smile at each prince, then look out at the audience even while she's concentrating on making the balance work in time with the music. Silly things can be distracting, like the fact that the men are wearing very long and elaborate cuffs, but worst of all is the fact that the Rose Adage has become so steeped in hype that it feels like make-or-break time whenever we dance it. More than with any other piece of choreography, we worry that if we do it badly we'll never get cast again. And having got wound up into a frenzy over it, some dancers just lose the plot of how to do a basic balance. It becomes a disaster on stage and the memories of it come back to haunt us all. I remember one Aurora who looked as if she was shaking hands with each prince because she'd panicked so badly she was unable to let go, and another who started to fall off point during a balance, grabbed at the prince and ended up doing a pirouette under his arm.

The thirty-two *fouetté* turns are another traditional nightmare. They come in Act III of *Swan Lake* and are danced by the Black Swan, Odile, as she's tricking Prince Siegfried into marrying her instead of the White Swan, Odette. They are a technical trick which some dancers can do much more easily than others, but everyone finds them horribly exhausting. (A few dancers simply can't do them and have to substitute another step, but that is always quite devastating to admit to.)

What makes the *fouettés* so daunting in this context is that they're all done on the left leg (with the right leg whipping round to the side) and they come straight after a solo, which is also nearly all on the left leg. So even before the ballerina has started on the *fouettés* that leg is already dying – and when you're tired, *fouettés* are very hard to control. You can easily get off the music, you can start to bang up and down off point instead of controlling your foot, and worst of all you can start straying all over the stage instead of turning on the spot. All you can do is keep smiling and try to convince the audience that you're enjoying yourself. Once I travelled so far forward that I ended up inches away from the orchestra, while my partner was setting off on a big circle of jumps around the stage. He was in a panic, not knowing if he should cross in front or behind me to avoid a collision, and finally I heard this desperate whispering, 'Go backwards, go backwards.'

At least in new ballets, audiences don't know the choreography so well and may not realize when something goes wrong. But on the opening night of Glen Tetley's ballet *Amores* my partner Stuart Cassidy and I had a disaster which few people could have missed. The ballet is very strenuous and ends with the visual climax of Cassidy lifting me high above his shoulders. This is a tricky moment because I have just stopped dead after a series of turns and he then has to just fling me up in the air. We'd managed the lift perfectly at every rehearsal but in the show it simply didn't happen. We were very hot and we may have been sweatier than usual, or we may have been over-confident or the timing may not have worked because we were tired. But his hands slipped out from under me and I didn't go anywhere. We couldn't substitute another step because it was the last chord of the music – so we just had to stand there hugging each other.

If dancers are having trouble with something in a *pas de deux* during rehearsal they often work out a cover-up version so that they can save themselves on stage. But some things we can't prepare ourselves for. One of my worst moments has to be the time I took a hard fall dancing Gamzatti in Natalia Makarova's production of *La Bayadère*. I was taking off for a big jump during the *pas de deux* and my foot slipped, so that I landed on my hip. I could hear the audience gasping and I blacked out briefly. I remember my partner, Johnny Cope, leading me off the stage because I'd lost all sense of direction, and it seemed to take a lifetime for us to reach the wings. Makarova was backstage and I remember her asking me over and over again, 'Darcey, Darcey, can you go back on stage?' I touched my leg and it had gone completely numb. Meanwhile, the *corps* were still having to go through their choreography without the *pas de deux* in front of them, wondering what on earth was going on. I thought I might just be able to do my solo, so I went back on stage and somehow I got through the steps.

My hip was so badly bruised that I couldn't stand the next day, but what made the experience unreal wasn't the pain, but the fact that every time my solo moved towards a different corner of the stage Makarova was always standing there, hissing, 'Go on, Darcey, you can do it.' I thought I was hallucinating; I couldn't understand how she could be standing everywhere at once. Sadly, but not surprisingly, I didn't finish the show.

The strangest moment in a performance has to be the time I blacked out while I was dancing Mitzi Caspar in Kenneth MacMillan's ballet *Mayerling*. It was in 1992, very soon after Kenneth had died so I'd been feeling very low, and obviously thinking about him a great deal. Suddenly I switched off from the moment so completely that I forgot what steps I should be dancing and had to repeat myself twice. It felt as though Kenneth had just tapped me on the shoulder to distract me. He always liked teasing his dancers, setting them tests, and it was as if he'd come back to play this little mental trick. I could imagine him up above me somewhere enjoying the moment, and saying,

'How are you going to recover from this?'

All these dramas go on during a show, but we're often barely aware of how the audience are responding. When we perform in big theatres, like Covent Garden, we feel very cut off from the public: the auditorium is a blank darkness in which we can just make out a few Exit signs and a wavy outline of heads, and we're concentrating so hard on our work that we can't even hear the audience clearly either. Even if they clap after a solo it sounds like a fuzz, and it's hard to tell whether there is genuine applause or just a polite spattering of claps.

All that we're directly aware of as we dance is the atmosphere, and that can vary a lot. Audiences which are very involved with what they're seeing give off a huge amount of energy. Even when people are quiet we sense it and feed off it. It's an amazing buzz. But those audiences tend to come at the end of the week when people are determined to have a good time. At the beginning of the week audiences are often less involved – they've just returned to work after the weekend and may not really want to be at the theatre. They feel very cold, very blank, and not open to suggestion. A good lively audience will always feel as if they are looking for something to enjoy. A bad audience can't be bothered.

So it's only at the end of the show that we can really assess what the public feel – and when they are genuinely enthusiastic the noise is incredible. It roars up at us and over us, like enormous waves crashing against rocks.

3

My Dancing Family –
Choreographers and
Partners

ONE OF THE most satisfying experiences we can have as dancers is performing a new role that's been created specially for us. No one else has ever danced it before and the steps fit like a glove. They have our personalities imprinted on them and because they've been made on our bodies we know that we can really dance them well.

But at the beginning of making any ballet, the dancers and the choreographer are often nervous of each other. It's a very intense relationship. We the dancers are the choreographers' raw material and they are not only making art out of us, they become something like our teacher, parent or lover. We want them to see something special in us, we want them to make something remarkable with us.

Some choreographers tend to respond to the most obvious qualities in the dancers they use. With me it's the size of my jump and the fact that I'm tall. But some like to work against the grain and invent more unexpected movements for us to dance, and that's always very exciting. Dancers constantly hope that a choreographer will discover some new aspect of themselves that's never been used before.

Because we're always in search of that excitement we don't tend to hold anything back during rehearsals. We want to show a choreographer everything we can do, and that puts us under a lot of physical strain. We are trying new things all the time, pushing our bodies to unknown limits, and this is very different from rehearsing the classics which are based on steps we do in class every day.

There's always a danger of injury when we work at this level of intensity. Choreographers have a habit of begging dancers to attempt a step 'just one more time please' and we aren't always good at looking after ourselves and saying no. When I first started working on Christopher Wheeldon's *Pavane* in 1996 I strained my thigh badly during one rehearsal from having to practise a particularly demanding step over and over again. The next day I found that I couldn't straighten my leg at all, which put me in a dilemma. I was obviously worried about doing some damage if I carried on rehearsing the step, but at the same time I didn't want to duck out of dancing properly. I hate being tame in rehearsals. If dancers are too protective of themselves when they're making a ballet it shows in the final work – it loses some of its excitement.

At the beginning of a new ballet dancers also have to get used to the way that the choreographer works, which can vary tremendously. Some choreographers walk into the studio for the first rehearsal and it's as if they have the whole ballet already worked out. I always think they must have the steps written down somewhere because they work so fast and appear to know so exactly what they are doing. Others, like Kenneth MacMillan, have very strong ideas about what they want but involve the dancers closely in the actual making of the steps. They get us to experiment with different ways of doing things, or even invent movements. This is very satisfying but it can put the dancers on the line both physically and emotionally. If they aren't experienced, they can feel nervous of making a fool of themselves.

All through rehearsals we are always watching the choreographer closely to see if he or she likes what we are doing. The problem is, they often don't know *themselves* and may let us carry on dancing in a certain way and then suddenly decide it's not right. And of course choreographers can get nervous too. The ballet may not be turning out the way they imagined, or they might worry that they're making steps which the dancers cannot physically do, and of course they are under pressure to finish on time. But we don't want choreographers to be nervous. We want them to be in control.

The most intense period I've ever spent with a choreographer was when I made *The Prince of the Pagodas* and *Winter Dreams* with Kenneth. I think some of the other dancers in the company were quite nervous for me when I started on *Pagodas* because Kenneth was renowned for pushing dancers hard to see how far they could go. He was interested to see what happened to people when they reached a breaking point – as if that was when they became most interesting and most creative. Some of the older dancers, who knew his reputation, were quite scared themselves of working on this ballet. I was only nineteen and very inexperienced, but it was an amazing time. With *Pagodas* the intensity and the excitement were more to do with creating the movement than the character. I had never choreographed anything myself so when Kenneth asked Johnny Cope and me to play around with ideas in our *pas de deux* I'd go wild trying out ideas which I had no notion whether I could do or not. I was discovering things about myself as a dancer that I didn't know before and it gave me a lot of freedom to express myself. But it was also quite nerve-racking. Kenneth may have liked to watch us experimenting but he also had a very strong concept of what his ballet should be, and after we'd tried out something we thought was really clever he'd get very impatient and shout, 'No, no,' or else he'd accept something one day and throw it out the next.

I was also intimidated by those early rehearsals because I'd never been partnered in a major role before – at Sadler's I had only danced solos – and I found the lifts and balances both physically scary and technically quite difficult. It often seemed to me that it was my fault when things went wrong.

At the end of rehearsals I frequently ran straight out of the studio and into the dressing room where I could burst into tears. I would never cry in front of Kenneth though. I sometimes felt that he was pushing me to cross some emotional line, that he wanted me to get upset, to wail or to rage, but during rehearsals I'd bottle up my emotions and I used to defuse the atmosphere by making Kenneth laugh. I wasn't consciously trying to stand up to him, I was simply protecting myself. Sometimes it annoyed him that I was being elusive and he used to scold me for running away after rehearsals because he liked to talk things over, but that period of making *Pagodas* was a busy time for me. It was in the middle of my first year with The Royal so I was learning a lot of new ballets, and I usually had another rehearsal to go to – I wasn't always running off to burst into tears of frustration.

I felt under a different kind of pressure, psychological rather than physical, when I started work on *Winter Dreams* with Irek Mukhamedov the following year. *Winter Dreams* began as a *pas de deux* which Kenneth choreographed for us soon after Irek left the Bolshoi and joined The Royal. I was still very young and inexperienced at the time, and was surprised that Kenneth had chosen me to be partnered by Irek, who was an international star. I assumed he would have wanted one of the older principals. But Irek had said he very much wanted to work with me; he'd seen me dancing on videos and astonished me by being very complimentary about my work.

Even so, I felt young and vulnerable working with both of

them. The ballet is based on Chekhov's play *The Three Sisters*. Irek was Vershinin, the ardent hero and I was Masha, the school teacher who is emotionally and sexually awakened by him. I realized that everyone was ready to see a lot of similarities between us and our characters, but I didn't feel confident about throwing myself into the role straight away.

Part of my problem was that I got very unnerved by Irek's acting during the early rehearsals. It felt as if he was trying to shock me because he was very passionate, kissing me for real which dancers normally never do in rehearsal! Kenneth loved it and obviously thought I was being too cool and too English when I didn't respond with the same heat. He kept goading me to get more passionate, asking me if I'd ever been in love and whether I had any idea what sexual passion was. Actually I *was* in love – I had my first serious affair when I was nineteen – but I didn't feel it was Kenneth's business and I wanted to keep some safe distance between us so I'd reply very coolly, 'Yes. I am in love.' It felt like a constant test.

I was also a very inexperienced actress in those days. *Winter Dreams* is a one-act ballet and its emotional climaxes occur very suddenly. Three years later when I came to dance Kenneth's *Romeo and Juliet* I found the acting very straightforward. The role builds much more slowly which means that I have a long time to get under Juliet's skin, and at the same time Prokofiev's music is incredibly moving. During performances I still often have tears running down my face.

But in *Winter Dreams*, crying was a humiliating struggle

for me. During one scene in the ballet Masha has to burst suddenly into tears and it felt natural for me to cover my face with my hands. Kenneth however wanted me to show all of Masha's emotion in my face and he kept nagging at me to act the scene in a different way. We argued and argued. I would say, 'But this is how I would cry' and he would say, 'Yes but I don't want to see *you* crying, I want to see *Masha* crying, and so do the audience. You have to show the public your face.' That taught me an important lesson about acting. I had always thought that if I felt natural performing a role it would also look more truthful, but that doesn't always work best on stage.

Once I'd gained my confidence though, working on this ballet was a transforming experience, especially being partnered by Irek. When I'd seen other Russian dancers on stage I'd thought their style was too similar to silent movie acting – it looked excessive. But when I danced with Irek he projected so much emotion, not just at the audience but at me, that I found it very natural to respond on the same level. It also helped that Irek was at that time a new and rather mysterious member of the company. It's harder to get passionate with someone with whom you've grown up.

English dancers often need help to get emotional on stage as it's not in our culture to do so, and working with Kenneth and Irek certainly taught me how to draw on my feelings while I danced. I think they helped me to express myself more openly in lots of ways.

Before I worked with Kenneth I had made one other ballet, David Bintley's *Spirit of Fugue*, which was a very different experience. David was very quiet and focused in the studio as he had quite a lot of the choreography worked out already and was anxious to get it all out in rehearsal. He was positive about what he liked and didn't like and we could actually spot the moments where he felt inspired, and where he seemed to be thinking, 'This is it. This is the picture I had in my head!' But he was also interested in what we could do as individuals, so he'd often incorporate spontaneous moments from rehearsals into the choreography as well. Once I did a very flukey move, something very difficult, which involved throwing my leg up and round in a *rond de jambe* while I was turning on point, and then repeating that move as I travelled backwards. I thought it would be impossible ever to do it again, but David said, 'Yes. Let's keep that in, you can do it again if we work on it.' I was often worried about keeping up with those kind of challenges but David didn't deliberately try to stir up our emotions like Kenneth, he was much more controlled and matter-of-fact.

It's fascinating learning about the personalities of new choreographers who come into the company from outside. The American choreographer Glen Tetley seemed a very alarming man the first time I worked with him, yet the second time he was a totally different person, gentle and controlled. My first encounter with him was in 1993 when he came into The Royal to stage his ballet *La Ronde*. This is a very cynical, very *fin de siècle* ballet which portrays a society obsessed by sex. It's an erotic chain dance in which each character moves on to have an affair with the next, and it's usually danced by principal artists. Unfortunately, an unusual number of dancers were injured at the time so our production had to have some *corps de ballet* dancers in its cast. Glen of course has a huge international reputation, he's made ballets for companies all around the world, and he expects to get the dancers he asks for. He jumped to the conclusion that the company weren't fully committed to him and so started off rehearsals in an angry frame of mind.

This was especially hard on those dancers who'd been substituted for his original choices – I think choreographers don't realize how quickly we sense that kind of thing. But even the principals had a bad time. I was cast as The Prostitute who opens and closes the ballet and I remember running my part every day over and over again. I was killing myself but I still couldn't please Glen. Some days he would just explode and walk out of the studio without giving any explanation.

But when he came back into the company four years later to create his new ballet *Amores* he was very different. This was an abstract work for six principals and he was pleased that he'd been given his first choice of dancers. Also, because we were a smaller group, he found it easier to communicate with us all. He loved to sit us down at the beginning of rehearsals and chat with us about his ideas. Many choreographers don't do this and it's a shame; if we get to know the choreographer and understand what he or she is after it's much easier to start rehearsals off on the right track.

Glen was always quite calm with us and softly spoken. But we could also see that he got incredibly frustrated sometimes because the style he wanted for this ballet was hard for us, as classical dancers, to grasp.

In ballet we are trained to make everything look as if it's the easiest thing in the world and we have to sustain this quality in our movements, even during class. We have to be perfectly on balance and we have to hold ourselves in very erect and dignified lines. There should be an openness across our chest and through our arms and all our movements should look as if they come from a very calm centre. But with Glen the movement was meant to look like agony, as if it was dragged from our guts. If he wanted us to curve our bodies backwards he'd tell us to feel as if someone was grabbing our insides and pulling them out. Some of it felt positively ugly to do and it was only when we saw the second cast dancing the ballet that we realized how well it actually worked.

For the six of us, as principal dancers, it was also quite an unusual experience to be working on a group piece like this. Normally we're dancing alone or in a couple and we have some freedom to interpret the choreography in our own, individual style. But with *Amores* we each had to be conscious of the other five dancers. Some of the choreography was in unison or in canon which I always find difficult as I tend to do steps slightly differently from other dancers. Mostly it's because I'm tall and have to restrict the scale of my movement to avoid getting out of line. During rehearsals for *Amores* we also had a few clashes of ego. One of us would say, 'Glen said he liked the way I did it,' and the rest would say, 'Yes, but I'm sure in the end we set it this way.'

It was certainly one of the hardest ballets I've ever danced, because it was so fast and strenuous. Once I fell to the floor in agony and I think that this was the moment when Glen finally felt I'd got the quality he wanted. Despite the fact that *Amores* didn't have a storyline we were meant to be projecting feelings of desperate hunger and desire.

Choreographers can be tricky about meaning. Glen told us that if we just danced his steps accurately then the meaning would emerge clearly through them. Many choreographers get impatient if you ask too many questions about what your role means, so I was intrigued when Twyla Tharp came into the company in 1995 to make her three-act ballet *Mr Worldly Wise* and gave me a book on the life of the American Shakers to read. She said it had influenced the philosophy of the ballet, particularly my role Truth on Toe, which was meant to symbolize the ideal which the main character (danced by Irek) was pursuing. When we work on any dramatic ballet we always read the play or book on which it's based, but I'd never had a choreographer talk to me about philosophy before.

Working with any choreographer involves an enormous element of trust because we have to give ourselves over to them so completely. We are their raw material and we have to trust that we won't be asked to dance anything that's too physically risky and that we aren't going to be made to look stupid. Sometimes that's hard to believe because of course we can't see the ballet from the outside. I remember in *Pagodas* Kenneth choreographed several moves where my arms were pulled into a very tightly constricted position. I felt as if I was the ugliest thing on stage. But I just had to believe that the effect was right.

Yet however much you have to trust your choreographer, your relationship with your partner is even more crucial. In the classics, most of the choreography for the principals is built around *pas de deux*, so the success or failure of a show depends on how well you're working with your partner. It's no good dancing your own steps perfectly, you have to work in harmony.

Of course both dancers are also putting their safety in each other's hands. For the woman the risk seems greatest because if a man drops her from a high lift or lets her fall off balance she looks at best ridiculous and can be seriously injured at worst. But the woman also has to look after the man, helping him when he lifts her so that she's not a dead weight which may strain his back. When you perform with a partner you're always hoping to make an ideal stage marriage, when the two of you are dancing together like one person.

So what makes a partnership work? In rehearsal it takes a lot of patience and a lot of give and take. One of you may be desperate to go over a *pas de deux* again and again to perfect something while the other is feeling bored, or pressured by a heavy work load. One of you may be feeling especially vulnerable to criticism, so the other may need to be particularly reassuring. One of you may have really strong ideas about how something should be done, but the other may have a different view. It's always crucial to let your partner get a word in, and I've had some bad clashes in rehearsals when I've been too quick to butt in with my helpful comments. It's essential to keep a sense of humour.

Johnny was the first partner I danced with in a major role and he probably knows me better than any other. He's looked after me and built up my confidence. To audiences all those high lifts and balances look so easy and airy, but when I first had to try them I was so terrified I really had to be pushed. The ground looks very far away when you're perched high above a man's head, and it's hard to believe that he's not going to drop you. But Johnny was always wonderful at explaining how lifts worked, and reassuring me that he knew exactly how to hold me.

When we first worked on *Pagodas* together he also taught me a lot about performing, just through the comments that he made during rehearsals. For instance he'd often remind me that I had to make all my steps as Princess Rose look beautiful. This made me quite indignant – of course I was trying to dance beautifully – but his point was that I had to do more than dance the steps, I had to look like a princess.

He also helped me to manage my nerves. About six months before we premièred *Pagodas* I danced my first principal role, Gamzatti, with him and I was so scared before each show that I always wanted to rehearse one of everything – a lift, a turn, a balance – just one time before the curtain went up. He'd be very cool and authoritative with me and say, 'No, Darce, you know you can do it, you've done it every rehearsal, you don't have to do it now.' The one time he *did* let me practise a turn I did it badly and he said, 'See, I told you. Now you'll go on stage thinking that you can't do it.'

Even now he's very good at relaxing me. He knows the right word to say when he sees that I'm winding myself up, not only before a show, but during performances too.

He's also very sensitive. He thinks I put myself down too much so he always makes a point of telling me if I'm doing something well. Just hearing 'Hey, that's really good, Darce' from him can do wonders for my dancing. Compliments from a partner are even better than compliments from a coach.

He and I have danced with each other for so many years now that in certain roles we can take risks and push each other to new dramatic heights. Once we performed four shows of *Romeo and Juliet* together – very rare in any season – and I've never felt so tuned in to a partner before. If I only have a couple of days rehearsing with a partner neither of us can move as far beyond the technique of the *pas de deux* as we'd like to. The audience may not notice, but we don't feel that we are giving one hundred per cent. When Johnny and I did those *Romeo and Juliet*s we were already technically confident together, so we could then focus on all the extra details of our performance such as holding our eye contact or finding moments where we could sustain a movement but still be together with the music. They are tiny nuances but they are what make a performance breathtaking.

Johnny is ideally suited to me because he's tall and strong, and it can be hard dancing with a man who isn't physically so right. Once I had to do two performances of MacMillan's *Song of the Earth* with Bruce Samson who is a beautiful dancer but quite slight in comparison with me. It was a last-minute cast change and we both knew that we weren't a good match. There are a couple of very strenuous lifts in the ballet, one where I'm upside down with my hands on his shoulders and he is pushing my legs vertically up in the air. While I was up there all I was thinking was 'Oh poor guy' and he was probably thinking 'Oh poor woman'. In fact we were able to make it work because we concentrated on getting the timing right and hearing the music together, which can be just as important to a lift as height and strength.

But sometimes these things aren't enough. After Irek and I had worked so well together in *Winter Dreams* everyone had very high expectations of us as a partnership and a few months later we were cast to dance in Kenneth's *Manon*. The problem was that while *Winter Dreams* had been created on the two of us, with all its steps tailored to our proportions, *Manon* had been created on two very different dancers: Antoinette Sibley and Anthony Dowell. They were not only smaller than us but also more similar to each other in build, and it soon emerged that I needed a partner taller than Irek to make the *pas de deux* in *Manon* work.

The problem was that no one admitted this early enough. At first we just couldn't figure out why so many steps seemed ridiculously difficult. Often it was just the small details that seemed impossible. At one moment I had to lean away from Irek's hip while he held me, and I couldn't get the right incline because I was too tall and his arm wasn't long enough. At another our cheeks weren't the right height to create the proper image. We kept trying and trying to make things work because there was so much riding on the show for both of us. We were dancing the first cast and *Manon* is one of the most important ballets Kenneth ever created.

But two weeks before the show it finally became obvious we couldn't do it, so I was pulled out of the ballet and Irek started to work with another principal, Viviana Durante. I felt completely rejected; I didn't see why *I* was the one who'd been pulled out of the ballet and why it was *I* who was being perceived as too tall instead of him as too short. I knew that Irek was a celebrity while I was at the beginning of my career, but at the same time I felt that, as the home-grown dancer, the company owed me more loyalty. I was angry no one had realized earlier that we weren't suited for *Manon* and even angrier that I wasn't allowed to dance the ballet that season with another partner. I threw a major tantrum, which is unlike me, and I had to wait for a couple of years before I finally got to dance the role.

Looking back, I now regard the whole fiasco as a learning experience – if a career doesn't have its downs as well as its ups you don't develop any mental toughness. But the event was made far more traumatic than it should have been by the overreaction of the press. My story made the front-page headline on one newspaper, right next door to a story about the Gulf War, which was just breaking out. It seemed crazy to me, but a lot of journalists had already decided that Irek and I were going to be the next Rudolf and Margot – another Russian and English dream team.

While the press and the public are always eager to spot new

partnerships in ballet, the dancers themselves are usually less willing to be paired off. Naturally if I dance a ballet with a superb partner then I want to do other roles with him, but I'd feel very limited if I could dance with no one else. It's usually such a buzz dancing with a new partner, especially in a romantic ballet like *Romeo and Juliet* – the first time I danced *Romeo and Juliet* with Igor Zelensky I was over-whelmed because he was so much more passionate on stage than he'd been in the studio. I also learn so much extra about a role by dancing it with different people. When a partner finds something new, or approaches the choreography in a different way, it gives me fresh inspiration and stops me getting stale.

When I first danced with Zoltan Solymosi, a Hungarian dancer who was with The Royal from 1992 to 1995 it was the greatest fun because, when he *liked* a role, he had such an appetite for performing. When he was on stage he was *definitely* on stage, and his excitement was infectious. When he was happy he could also communicate a fantastic confidence. When I first danced Balanchine's *Tchaikovsky Pas de Deux* with him (in 1991) I could tell exactly how the movements should feel and how they should look as soon as he took hold of me. There are several risky moves in it, like flying leaps where the woman is caught by her partner, and I felt utterly safe with him.

Unfortunately when Zoltan hated a role, like the Prince in *Sleeping Beauty*, he really let me know it. He'd get nervous and frustrated and become so preoccupied with his own feelings that he'd lose his concentration partnering.

Physically that made me feel insecure because I'd never know what he was about to do, but it would also make the role feel dramatically wrong. We'd be celebrating our wedding in Act III of *Beauty* but instead of being the radiant bride I would be having to keep a wary eye on him.

During the last few years I've performed many shows with Igor Zelensky, who was trained with the Kirov, then danced with New York City Ballet and now guests all over the world. I've danced with him in London and also in galas abroad and he's certainly become one of my favourite partners. He makes me feel so confident that he brings out qualities in me that no one else can find.

One reason is that he's extremely strong, so I never have to worry about my height or my own physical strength. But he's psychologically strong too so there's no question of over-powering him in rehearsal. Igor is not only very positive about what he wants from a role, he's also highly professional so he's always happy to rehearse a *pas de deux* over and over again. He doesn't mind me making suggestions either which is a big advantage as I'm always much too quick to open my mouth. I'm always seeing different ways of making a step work and saying things like, 'Don't you think it would be really good if you did this or that?' With some people I have to learn to be tactful and wait a few seconds before butting in, but Igor doesn't take offence.

I love the fact too that in performance he always wants to get out on stage and do a great show. It's very discouraging to be with a partner who's feeling so nervous or wound up that he just wants the show to be over. I've got into states like that myself, when all I'm thinking is that I want to be at the end of Act III, but it's a terrible thing to do to your partner and so far Igor has never done it to me. He's a perfectionist and he wants to get as much as he can out of each show.

Technically we were suited to each other from the start, but we didn't discover how well we worked dramatically until we danced *Romeo and Juliet* in London for the first time. Igor was a revelation. He was actually quite nervous before the first show because he felt he hadn't had enough time to learn the role, so there were moments on stage where I was having to reassure him. But at other moments he was extraordinarily passionate and he did some things with such force – like grabbing my hand or running across the stage or kissing me – that I was nearly knocked over.

Kissing on stage can often be a surprise because most dancers (with the exception of Irek) tend not to rehearse kisses in the studio. There's more of a charge if you wait until the performance, although in most ballets you can't actually kiss too passionately as there's so much else going with the choreography and the music, plus you're both covered in heavy stage make-up.

Some dancers talk all through a show, which I dislike, but I do make comments when it's necessary. If the music is going at a strange pace my partner and I will be muttering to each other – 'It's going slow here, no, no it's getting fast again' – or if something like a pirouette has gone wrong and the man is obviously getting frustrated I will always say reassuring things like, 'It's fine, it's fine. We can make up for it by the end.'

When I was first partnered by Adam Cooper (who later left The Royal and became a star with the modern dance theatre company Adventures in Motion Pictures) he was horribly nervous and couldn't stop shaking, which was obviously scary for me. But when he overcame his nerves he became a very good partner. I loved dancing *Romeo and Juliet* with him because he acted with such an honest passion; I felt as if there was a real person there when he looked at me, he was never playing games. Adam also became a wonderfully reliable substitute, who was brilliant at standing in at the last minute if another guy was injured, and there have been several shows when I've said a prayer of thanks for him.

I remember one potentially disastrous show of *Pavane* where he certainly performed miracles. The day started off badly because I'd been kept awake most of the previous night by a stomach bug, so during the afternoon I went to the Green Room to try and catch a little sleep. There I met Johnny, who was meant to be partnering me that evening, and who told me that I should go home and have a proper rest. My flat was quite a long drive from the Opera House so I said no, it was too much effort. Then I said, 'It's OK for you, you can just jump onto your motorbike and you're home in two seconds.'

I should never have had this conversation however, because at five o'clock that afternoon I heard that Johnny *had* gone home on his motorbike to rest before the show but had had an accident on the way back. I thought, 'Oh my God, I've jinxed him.' Fortunately he wasn't seriously injured because he'd managed to jump off the bike before he was hit. But he had strained his thumb and cracked his rib and certainly couldn't partner me that night.

This was only the second performance of *Pavane* I'd ever danced so I wasn't very confident about the ballet anyway. To complicate matters there was only one other man who knew Johnny's role, which was Adam, and I'd never rehearsed *Pavane* with him. But worst of all no one knew how to get hold of Adam and break it to him that he had to partner me that night.

We looked at the schedule and saw that he was due to come into the Opera House at 5.30 for a costume fitting. But the show started at 7.30 so we would barely have time to go through the choreography together. *Pavane* isn't an easy *pas de deux* to switch partners in at the best of times; it had taken Johnny and me ages to get some of the steps right because so much was left to chance in the choreography. In one promenade he'd only be supporting me because my arms were round his neck which meant that if I was a fraction off balance he couldn't save me at all.

When we finally tracked Adam down he acted very cool and said, 'Oh OK, fine.' At least we had an hour left to run through the ballet, but during that time we discovered that Adam had been handling quite a lot of the choreography differently with his own partner (Chloe Davies) from the way Johnny and I had danced. He didn't know exactly what I'd be doing in certain moves, nor I him.

Of course the company made an announcement to the audience before we went on stage so that they knew Adam had stepped into the role at the last minute, but it didn't make me feel much better. I didn't believe the public could really understand what it meant that we'd never worked together on this ballet at all.

When the curtain went up I was trembling all over and I could only get through the ballet by concentrating on one step at a time. I'd finish one and think, 'OK, that's done. Now here's the next one, what have I got to think about now? I must make sure I do this.' Amazingly it went all right apart from one sticky moment in an arabesque turn where Adam was holding my hand much tighter than Johnny ever had and I panicked that he'd never let go. Otherwise he was fantastic, responding very quickly to what I was trying to do, so if I went slightly off balance he'd sense it straight away and save me much more quickly than most other men could. It didn't matter how much was thrown at him, he always seemed to survive.

But for the next crisis of that season, even Adam abandoned me – in fact my partners seemed to be falling over like a stack of dominoes. The drama blew up during the final rehearsals for our revival of *Pagodas*, which was two weeks after the *Pavane* trauma. I was meant to be dancing the first night with Johnny but after his motorbike accident this was out of the question, so the obvious replacement was Adam. He was the right height for me and I'd once danced the ballet with him six years previously.

Still, the change of partners was an alarming prospect. We only had six days to get the ballet working for us which is a very short time for a three-act show, especially one with so many difficult *pas de deux* in it, and our very first rehearsal

94

together was actually a stage call. This was very unsettling as usually, by the time we're rehearsing on stage, we're dancing a ballet straight through – we're not trying to work things out with a brand-new partner.

We got through the ballet more or less, but then, when I went in for my second rehearsal with Adam, I discovered that he'd been pulled from *Pagodas* and been recast as Sylvie Guillem's partner in *Romeo and Juliet*. Sylvie's original Romeo had been Johnny and as soon as she'd heard about his accident she had tried to contact Laurent Hilaire, her old partner from Paris Opéra, to replace him. Unluckily Laurent couldn't make that date so Sylvie was insisting that Adam dance with her instead. For contractual reasons, what Sylvie wanted, Sylvie got.

Since Sylvie's Juliet was scheduled two days before the opening of *Pagodas* it was clearly impossible for Adam to rehearse with her as well as with me. So Anthony Dowell decided that I would have to be partnered by Cassidy instead.

To do Anthony justice he looked very nervous as he told me but I was still very, very upset. I thought that if Sylvie needed another partner she should find one herself and not take mine. I was furious too because the changes would be so traumatic for everyone else involved. Cassidy was going to have a hard time partnering me because he'd been rehearsing *Pagodas* with Miyako Yoshida, who is half my height. Miyako was going to suffer because Cassidy would have to cancel his rehearsals with her, even though she was making her own début as Princess Rose and needed all the preparation time she could get. Finally, Adam would be under horrible pressure. One minute he was rehearsing *Pagodas* with me and the next he'd been given two days to rehearse *Romeo and Juliet* with Sylvie. He hadn't danced the ballet for about three years – though being Adam he managed to perform miracles on the night.

Meanwhile I was worrying that I should be fighting harder for my own rights, and simultaneously fretting that it would be selfish for me to do so. There was no doubt that Adam was a better partner for me than Cassidy, since Cassidy wasn't an ideal height for me in *Pagodas* and besides we'd only danced one ballet together before, which was *Sleeping Beauty*. Despite all the hard work I'd put into rehearsing *Pagodas* I knew that I wouldn't look as good as I should. It was so frustrating, I wondered if I should stamp and scream and insist on Adam.

But I could also see the dilemma Anthony was facing. Adam was the only other man with whom Sylvie had ever danced in the company and it was impossible for her to do *Romeo and Juliet* with Cassidy because he was too short for her. If I threw a tantrum it wouldn't help the situation at all because we'd simply miss a day's rehearsal, which we couldn't afford to do. Plus I have always felt uncomfortable having scenes; I end up in tears and, unlike Sylvie who can come in and out of the company, I have to live with everyone. So finally and reluctantly I agreed.

As I predicted, rehearsals were rocky for both Cassidy and me. Our bodies weren't ideally suited and none of the *pas de deux* worked naturally for us. But amazingly when it came to the show, it went quite well and one particular lift in Act III which had been a nightmare at every rehearsal turned out perfectly. I remember seeing a look of huge relief on the faces of the *corps de ballet* at the side of the stage and hearing a collective gasp of delight. So that made up for some of the trauma.

It's such an intense and intimate experience performing a three-act ballet with a partner, however many problems we may have weathered during rehearsals. We both start off feeling apprehensive but then as we get into the show I can feel the man change. He's not holding on to me so tightly, and he's feeling my weight more accurately as I make transitions into lifts or promenades. We start to transmit an amazing amount of information between us and it becomes a simultaneous performance – we're dancing as one person. There are some dancers who seem so wrapped up in themselves that they look as if they could virtually dance the show on their own. But they are missing out on what is, for me, one of the most intimate and exciting challenges of being a ballet dancer.

4

MY FAVOURITE ROLES

BALLET HAS BECOME an international art, with foreign tours taking up part of nearly every company's schedule, and individual dancers jetting around the world to make guest appearances. I like to guest myself as I'm always intrigued to see how other companies operate and it's exciting to appear before different audiences. Occasionally companies even ask me to stay. But one reason why The Royal feels like home to me, and why I'd hate to leave, is that it has such a wide repertoire. We perform more ballets than almost any other company in the world, and this means we're not only encouraged to dance a wide variety of styles, but we can also act out very different roles on stage. We can be a princess one day, a prostitute the next or just a pure dancer in motion.

The great nineteenth-century classics like *Sleeping Beauty* and *Swan Lake* are the basis of The Royal's repertory and they are essential for dancers because they demand such pure classical technique. Even though each company might perform a slightly different version of the Petipa and Ivanov classics the core of the choreography remains the same. The steps are handed down from generation to generation and they are as important to us as class. But we also perform many twentieth-century ballets, including some very modern works by choreographers like William Forsythe which push our bodies into unknown territory. Then we have a number of dramatic ballets by, for instance, Frederick Ashton and Kenneth MacMillan, which most dancers love because they require us to act as well as to dance.

If I had to choose a favourite work it would be Kenneth MacMillan's *Romeo and Juliet*, which he choreographed in 1965, but which we still perform nearly every season. It's possible to play dramatically with this ballet so much, and it feels very different to performing the nineteenth-century classics. When I'm dancing Aurora I have to concentrate on the technical challenges of the role, but when I dance Juliet I become totally carried away with the music; I forget about technique and about everybody else, and when I come off stage at the end I don't feel critical the way I do after most performances. Usually all the things that I've done wrong depress and irritate me, but with Juliet I just come offstage and sigh.

A lot of people assume it must be a difficult ballet to act because Juliet has to grow up so much, she has to change from being a young girl into a woman. She's virtually a child when she comes on in Act I but Prokofiev's music and Kenneth's choreography are so dramatically entwined that they create the character for you. Every step, every gesture and every pause have been so cleverly timed that it's easy to feel all the uncertainty and spontaneity of a very young girl.

At the very beginning of the ballet Juliet is totally oblivious to the significance of what's going on around her. Her choreography is very playful and springy as she's darting around between moods. When Paris is presented to her by her parents she looks at him very curiously but she soon loses interest and goes back to playing with her Nurse. Then she starts to get a bit self-conscious with these adults around her and realizes that the situation is more grown up than she thought. It's a little threatening and she loses her nerve, so she *bourrées* in a tight circle around her Nurse and tries to hide behind her. The Nurse is Juliet's security blanket, she's looked after her since she was a baby and Juliet thinks if she clings to her then maybe these adults will go away and stop watching her.

When they've finally left, Juliet tries to go back to playing with her doll but the Nurse tells her that this visit from her suitor means she has to start thinking about growing up. Juliet touches her breasts and suddenly understands it's true. Everything is going to change, she's going to be a woman. The music which accompanies this gesture makes it feel like a very significant moment. Sometimes the audience laugh because it's almost as if Juliet has only just discovered that she has breasts, but that never distracts me. Juliet's so excited, she's feeling, 'Wow, I'm going to be a woman like my mother. I could be attractive and I might start to be attracted to a man. I've got all this exciting grown up stuff waiting for me.'

In the ball scene Juliet has become more like an awkward teenager. When she comes on stage she's the centre of attention but she doesn't want to be there at all. She doesn't know how to act and she's desperate for something to hang on to. She feels better when she's given a definite role to play, like the moment when Paris takes her by the hand and leads her round, or when she has to play her mandolin to everyone. Then she's thinking, 'Oh yes, I can handle this. I've been watching other people do this for years,' because of course Juliet comes from a rich and noble family. She has a strong sense of public occasion.

Then she starts to sense that Romeo is staring at her and even though he has a mask on he's like a magnet, she becomes attracted to him with every nerve. This is when the role starts to get really exciting because I can build up so much tension just by being totally motionless while everyone else is moving around the stage. It's eerie how you can make yourself the focus of the whole theatre's attention by being the still point on a busy stage.

But I don't feel as if I'm acting here. I've *become* Juliet because I'm letting myself re-experience all the feelings that I've had in real life when someone I've been attracted to has come close to me. I remember how electric the air became, and how all I was conscious of was their physical presence. This is the lovely thing about dancing Juliet. We can all identify with her because she's not a magical princess, she's a real teenager and we've all been where she is.

When Juliet first dances with Romeo it's a very brief encounter. But as soon as he starts to hold her it's as if they are drawn into their own private shell, she only has eyes for him. At this moment she has definitely started to grow up. She begins to realize that she has some control over this situation and she feels like a woman. But she's also very innocent still, so when Romeo comes very close to her it's too much. She draws back – he's still a stranger and she's still very naïve – and it's important not to let Juliet grow up sexually too fast. You have to build it up slowly so that her feelings can really explode in the bedroom scene in Act III.

Of course the balcony scene at the end of Act I is also a big climax for her. All the way through it Juliet is understanding more and more about what it is she's feeling. She's experiencing all these little rushes of emotion as she realizes that she and Romeo know each other a hundred times better than they did a few seconds ago. The moment when she looks him full in the face is terribly exciting for her; they have nothing left to hide from each other.

The choreography is quite demanding in this scene but it has to look as if it's being driven purely by the characters' feelings and the music, and that it's no effort for the dancers. There's one point where Romeo is on his knees and Juliet is dotting around him in these little jumps and the choreography isn't saying – as it might be in a classic – 'Look how clever I am, I can jump so lightly on one foot,' but 'I'm floating in ecstasy around my new lover.'

The lifts are also hard to get right technically because they require a very dreamy quality. Again, nothing can appear to be an effort. Romeo and Juliet have to look as if they are perfectly matched and that they are melting into each other's bodies. It's crucial to get the timing exact too: at every moment the dancers have to be right up on the beat, as if the music is lifting them. In the classics the timing is much more measured and comfortable, but in this *pas de deux* if we aren't on the rise of the music the whole time it doesn't communicate the surge of emotion which our characters are feeling.

The mood is very ecstatic but not really erotic yet, so when Romeo kisses Juliet she touches her lips, as if she's still trying to understand the sensation. Her back arches away from his embrace and she breaks his touch. Her feelings are so powerful that they drag her away from him, they are too overwhelming for her to bear any more.

By the time they get to the bedroom scene Juliet's absolutely crazy for him, and it's dreadful for her because she knows that he's going to leave. She's maddened by a horrible needy desire to latch on to him, so she throws herself at his leg to try and stop him going. I always feel wound up to a pitch of extreme erotic tension here, even though Juliet's actions are almost childlike.

Then her parents walk in to tell her that she must marry Paris and she feels dizzy because so much is happening to her and she's having to grow up so quickly. From the skittish child she was in Act I, she's become a woman who knows exactly what she wants – and it's Romeo. But her tragedy is, she can't tell anyone. I always feel here that Juliet is dying to tell her mother but she knows that it would explode the situation into a crisis so she can't.

To me it's agony that Juliet is forced to be so alone and so silent because when I'm upset or anxious in real life I always need to talk. Even if someone can't give me any answers I feel better having talked about my problems. Juliet can't turn to her Nurse, who's always helped her before, and her mother doesn't understand her situation at all. Even so Juliet runs to her mother and begs her, 'Please, you must understand, you must know what's going on.' But then Paris comes up behind her and the moment for throwing herself on her mother's mercy has passed. She's revolted by Paris, 'Ugh, he's touching me again,' and she really hates him; when she first saw him she thought he was perfect, but that was before she'd met Romeo.

Finally Juliet's parents leave her and at this point I'm always crying on stage. I suppose it's because my own biggest terror is being abandoned. I have a fear that some day my friends and family won't be there for me and I always think that one of the hardest parts of growing up is the discovery that our parents aren't the perfect, powerful beings we thought they were. They're normal people, who won't always make the right decisions for us and protect us, and that's the pain that Juliet's experiencing. She still badly wants to please her parents yet they, devastatingly, are refusing to help her, so suddenly she's on her own.

At this point she's completely alone on stage and she has to communicate all this rush of thought and emotion through mime. Each gesture has to be made very carefully with the music in order to work up the tension. Juliet circles the floor and goes to the door. Her scarf is there and she clutches it to her. It's another security blanket and it gives her courage. Then she goes and sits on the bed and this is where she realizes that she has to get herself together if she wants to see Romeo again. There are no gestures here to convey what she's thinking, only the music, which builds to a very emotional pitch. I can actually feel the sound inside me as I sit there, staring out at the darkness; it's such a powerful sensation that it lifts me up through my back, and if I get the timing right then the audience can see it too.

As Juliet sits there completely motionless on an empty stage, it's a very long moment in ballet terms. Audiences aren't used to nothing happening, but to the dancer it actually doesn't feel long enough as so much is going through Juliet's mind and she's growing up so profoundly. Then suddenly she is up and running off to Friar Lawrence, and the sudden shift into action feels like a wonderful release.

I remember that when I watched Gelsey Kirkland dancing Juliet while I was still a student I initially thought that she performed this run in too extreme and stylized a manner. With her cloak floating out behind her and her legs flying up in front of her she hardly seemed to touch the floor. Art can so easily become comic when you aren't completely absorbed into the moment. But then I saw that she'd made the character of Juliet so real that this run had nothing to do with dance technique. It was like a symbol of

Juliet's love, possessing her and making her incredibly powerful.

When I first started dancing Juliet myself in 1993 the side of her character that I found most difficult to identify with was the way she flies off the handle so abruptly. In real life I tend to contain myself. When I get upset or angry I take a deep breath. But Kenneth wanted Juliet to be constantly veering from one emotional extreme to another, in order to show the audience all that she is going through. In the bedroom scene for instance she's like a child at one moment, wanting to hit Romeo because he says he has to leave, then suddenly she's turned passionate and tender again and would do nothing to hurt him.

In the scene where her parents return to confront her again with Paris Juliet is really bouncing off the walls. She's decided that she will take the potion which Friar Lawrence has given her which means that she knows she can safely agree to marry Paris. She'll be totally unconscious on the morning of her wedding day and everyone will think she is dead. But despite this plan she still hates Paris. She's revoltingly stubborn, she can't bear to agree to even a sham engagement. When he tries to partner her she refuses to look at him, she is so furious she behaves like a spoilt brat.

I love performing this scene because it allows me to get so angry. Paris is holding on to Juliet and she's pulling away from him, her body all stubbornly limp and unresponsive. It's actually quite a hard way to dance because it requires maintaining the strength in our legs and stomach while still looking floppy. Of course Juliet's resistance makes Paris angrier and angrier, as he looks such a fool, so when Juliet breaks away and runs to the corner of the stage he chases after her. He's probably going to slap her. But then she suddenly turns on him and the mood snaps. She's looking him straight in the eyes, possessed with rage and dismay and he's utterly shocked by her. When I dance this scene with Christopher Saunders he always makes Paris look very upset and bewildered at this point. He's been trying to force Juliet to accept him but then he realizes how vulnerable and unhappy she is, and he starts to think he shouldn't push her any more. So then Juliet feels slightly sorry for him; she walks slowly back and finishes the *pas de deux*. She says she'll marry him but she's still giving him absolutely nothing.

The scene where Juliet takes the potion is rather like the mad scene in *Giselle*. Her imagination is running wild and she's miming a very rapid sequence of thoughts and feelings. She reaches out for the bottle then throws it down on the floor and goes back to her bed. Then she stands up slowly and says to herself, 'I'm going to take it this time.' So she moves sideways towards the bottle like a crab, which feels very unnatural but shows the audience exactly how frightened Juliet is feeling.

Again, the timing of this scene is crucial. The tension has to be built very slowly, right up to the point where Juliet pulls the stopper off and gulps the potion down. Some dancers prefer to act even this moment slowly – they stare at the bottle before they drink – but I always feel that Juliet has absolutely willed herself to do it. It's now or never.

When you've drunk the potion, you touch your mouth

and neck and you can feel it running down your throat like liquid lead. You're swallowing hard, and because you've just been moving around your heart is going boom boom boom, so the moment feels very real. Then Juliet is sick – and dancers have very different views on how she should do this! Some jerk their hand out in front of them as they are sick, as if to show the vomit running over their fingers and force everyone to see how revolting it is. Others jerk their hand against their mouth as if Juliet is trying to hold the vomit in – she's terrified of sicking up the potion in case it doesn't work. Whichever way you do it you have to let yourself look really ugly in this scene; if you look too classical you're not telling the audience enough. When I fall to the floor after I've drunk the potion I always end up with bruises on my knees. As a dancer you're always told not to hurt yourself but I can't help it. I just crash down.

Then there is the agony of trying to crawl back up onto the bed. There isn't a lot of music for this because the scene changes to the next one where Juliet's friends come in to try and wake her. But it's surprisingly hard to get up there in time. The bed is very high and you are trying to haul yourself up onto it while looking as if you've lost all the strength in your limbs. Worse still, you are desperately trying to make sure that you aren't standing on the skirt of your dress. The shoulder straps on this costume are very elastic and if you catch your skirt as you climb you pull the bodice right down to your waist.

So you're trying to mime that you are terrified and in pain while also trying to keep yourself decent. At the same time you're having to make the audience understand why Juliet is trying to get back up on the bed anyway. She could just stay on the floor but she's desperate to reach the window out of which Romeo climbed, so that she can feel close to him when the potion starts to work.

In the final scene, where Juliet wakes up to find herself in the tomb, there are some similarly tricky moments when you're having to persuade the audience of the truth of what you're doing, even though Juliet's actions don't seem at all logical. For instance, when she awakes and sits up it would be obvious for her to see the bodies of Romeo and Paris straight away. After all, they are lying in the middle of the stage. But first Juliet has to show the audience the horror of the tomb and to make them feel how overwhelmingly cold and dark it is. So she steps over Paris and goes to the back of the stage to take in the whole scene and only then does she suddenly sense that Romeo is there – and she turns round and sees him immediately.

Once she's discovered that he's dead she has to stab herself, and that can give dancers some very bad moments. Juliet is meant to use Romeo's knife but sometimes it's impossible to see where it has fallen on the stage after his fight with Paris. So then you have to look around for Paris' knife instead. I had one very nerve-racking show when I couldn't see either. I looked frantically around and finally spotted a faint shape right at the edge of the stage. I prayed that it was a knife and moved towards it – and luckily it was. But during that split second I was having to wonder what I would do if it wasn't. I'd have to improvise another way of dying, but what? I could have tried strangling myself or banging my head against the tomb! I could have fallen off the tomb and knocked myself out! But it wouldn't have been a very tragic or dignified death!

Even at the point of death Kenneth still gives Juliet a few problems, because after she has stabbed herself she makes the apparently masochistic choice of climbing right *up* and *over* the tomb even though she's in agony. It's crucial to make the audience understand that Juliet cannot bear to die without Romeo, which is why she is crawling this long way back to him. The moment can feel as if it lasts for ever, but if you know the music well then you can make it work for you, because it's expressing the depth of Juliet's love and sorrow. There's a motive for every step in the music which is why Juliet feels as real to me as I hope she does to the audience.

Another ballet in which I've similarly lost all sense of myself in a role is Kenneth's *Song of the Earth*. The power of this ballet took me by complete surprise when I first danced it in 1990 as it doesn't have a detailed plot or characters like *Romeo and Juliet*. But it is set to a song cycle by Mahler, whose lyrics describe the process of death separating a woman from the man she loves, and the music itself is painfully moving in parts. When I danced the role of The Woman I was still very young, and I was physically and emotionally overpowered by it.

Even though The Woman isn't a fully developed character, the role makes it clear that she's always aware of

Death's power to ruin her life and that she is much more clear-sighted about this than her lover is. So every time the choreography forces Death between her and The Man she not only feels the agony of their parting for herself, she feels it for both of them. Her pain builds up in the choreography and the music until the last duet, where she *bourrées* down stage with her back towards the audience, then falls into The Man's arms. The first time I ever performed the role I felt genuinely broken-hearted at this point; I couldn't bear the fact that this was going to be my last moment with my lover. I was also in a state of total physical exhaustion because I'd thrown myself so completely into the choreography, and when I came offstage I had the strangest sensation of not knowing where I was or what I'd just been doing. I had been so totally wrapped up in the ballet that I was completely wrung out and disoriented.

I don't know if I'd be so overpowered by the role now, simply because I'm older and less able to throw myself so recklessly into my dancing. I've had some serious injuries since then and I have to take care of myself. But I still feel a close affinity with Kenneth's works – I always feel very passionate when I dance them, especially the two roles he created for me.

The Prince of the Pagodas was the first of course, and even when we came to revive it, six and a half years later, I found that the choreography was still in my body. I could remember the steps very easily and they felt very special to me. Also, as Johnny and I were rehearsing we kept remembering all the comments Kenneth used to make. At any moment we expected him to walk into rehearsals the way he always used to, rather slow and laid back, but with someone or other always buzzing around him asking questions. Even though he'd become physically quite frail by the time he made *Pagodas* his mind was always very active. We'd always be wondering how Kenneth was going to tease us that day, what kind of things he was going to ask of us. Coming back to the ballet, it was so hard to believe that he wasn't alive any more.

Pagodas is an epic piece to dance and at the end, although I don't feel emotionally wrung out the way I do after Juliet, I am physically shattered. I feel as if I've run a marathon or been beaten up. There's a lot of choreography for my role, Princess Rose, and it's technically hard to dance despite the fact that a lot of the steps look simple. Kenneth based the ballet on *Sleeping Beauty* so he wanted the movement to look especially clean and precise – as though it were a nineteenth-century classic. But it's much sparer than the choreography for *Beauty* and as there are none of those little Petipa steps which you can do quickly, one after the other, it's much harder to cover up any mistakes.

Being Kenneth, too, the choreography is full of odd or unexpected effects. In my Act I solo I have to come out of a big jump and hold my landing position for a beat – which is tricky – before going into a turn. In the Act III *pas de deux* there are some lifts which make me feel as if I'm being turned inside out because the positions are so odd. During one of them, my partner has to hold me up high above his shoulders but with my arms pulled tightly behind me, so I feel very off-balance and constricted.

Some people assume *Pagodas* must also be hard to dance because Britten's score sounds difficult compared to the more familiar Tchaikovsky and Prokofiev ballet music. I know that the *corps de ballet* had problems at first because a lot of the dancers were hearing the music in different ways which made it hard for them to dance together. But the music for my solos and *pas de deux* is some of the most beautiful in the score and it's straightforward to hear and count. The only section I had problems with was my Act II solo which Kenneth set very rigidly on the beat. My instinct was to dance *through* the music but at this point Rose is being threatened by the Four Kings who want to seduce her and gain her father's kingdom, so Kenneth wanted my dancing here to look very nervous and staccato.

Pagodas is one of Kenneth's most abstract story ballets. He based it on several other fairy tales as well as *Beauty* and he wanted the plot to be a kind of distillation of them all. When we first started to make the role he told me to think in terms of Aurora, but he also wanted me to put a lot of myself in. He'd chosen me in the first place because he thought my personality was very like his heroine – a very young and naïve princess who is willing to put up with an awful lot being thrown at her!

He didn't create such a detailed dramatic script as he did for characters like Juliet or Manon, which left me a lot of room to include my own reactions and feelings. This made the role very easy for me but very hard for some of the other dancers who have performed it. Kenneth even had too much music for certain sections (it's a very long score) and there are some brief unchoreographed gaps between Rose's solos or *pas de deux* which the dancer has to fill herself. The hardest is where Rose is alone on an empty stage after the Fool has left her and she's basically just rushing from one corner to another, wondering what she should do. I know exactly what she's thinking at this point because I talked about the ballet so much with Kenneth and I relish having the stage to myself for a change. But dancers who don't know what they are meant to be expressing tend to dither around a little.

When I first performed the role I used to shake all the way though sections of it and by Act III I'd be exhausted and dreading the final *pas de deux* which involves some of the trickiest moves in the whole ballet. There's one moment where I'm flying towards the Prince in a high *jeté* and he has to catch me. When Johnny does this he always likes to walk away from me rather than standing still so that he can catch me at the last possible moment. During one performance I nearly yelped, he looked such a terrifyingly long distance away from me, and when he caught me the whole stage (and probably the audience) gasped with relief.

Moments like that are scary but they're also what make performing fun. Even though the choreography of *Pagodas* looks quite classical it's possible to play around with the steps. There are always new ways of making transitions between moves, or slightly different ways of dancing with the music, or new points of emphasis to find. That freedom is what keeps a role alive.

I also love dancing Masha in Kenneth's *Winter Dreams*

although I find it much harder to build up her character than I do that of Juliet or Princess Rose. It's only a one-act ballet, which means there is simply less time to develop the role, and also the action is structured in a very bitty fashion. I spend quite a lot of the ballet sitting behind a gauze screen rather than being on stage, which gives me too much time to worry about what's coming next and not enough time to get involved in my character. But when I *am* dancing I find that every step expresses exactly what Masha is thinking and feeling. In some ballets, the choreography goes at a leisurely pace with sequences of mime alternating with sections of very technical dancing. But in *Winter Dreams* it's all very compressed. Even though some of the moves feel quite strange to perform, because they are tense and awkwardly shaped, I can physically experience all of Masha's frustration as I dance it, the sense that she's trapped and unable to reveal her feelings.

The Royal Ballet's other great choreographer is Frederick Ashton but for a long time I felt quite distant from his work. I always thought 'Sir Fred's not for me.' His ballets are very lyrical, while I was always regarded as a technical dancer with a lot of attack, and his ballerina roles tend to be danced by smaller women. But as I've grown older my dancing has become more lyrical, and from the moment I first danced in Ashton's *Cinderella* in 1993 I felt completely natural in it.

Even though the role is less dramatically involving than Juliet, it has a fairy-tale quality which feels magical to dance. There's also a lot of fun in it, especially when Cinderella is squabbling with her Ugly Sisters, where Ashton gives the ballerina quite a lot of freedom to play with the role. Personally, I don't allow Cinderella to get too pathetic, so even though the choreography doesn't allow her to confront the Ugly Sisters I like her to get angry with them when they really push her around. And I like her to be a bit sparky too. Although Cinders is meant to have a downtrodden life by the fireside, I think of her as having a good time.

These kitchen scenes may be fun but they are also quite confusing to perform. There are a lot of props involved, and the kitchen scene in Act I is disconcertingly similar to the one in Act III. This means that I'm always worrying whether I should be picking up a piece of material or a broom or whether I'm meant to be looking at my mother's picture.

I also don't enjoy the fact that the choreography in Act I involves dozens of tiny *bourrées* which kill my feet. Basically these are small running steps on point, during which you have to give the illusion that your feet and legs stay very close together. The reason why I find *bourrées* hard is that I have very bendy feet which makes it hard for me to stay right on the tips of my toes. My weight tends to tip forward so I've had to learn to compensate by leaning slightly back. I also have long feet and long legs which means that there is simply more of me to co-ordinate than there is in smaller dancers. I've noticed how other tall dancers have developed their own idiosyncratic ways of getting around the *bourrée* problem. Sylvie, for example, does hers with her weight nearly all on the back foot and with her back leg slightly turned in. It looks odd from the wings but fabulous from out front.

There are a lot of *bourrées* in the ballroom act too, but otherwise the choreography is bliss. Prokofiev's music makes me feel deliciously sparkly and there's a wonderful flow to the way Ashton co-ordinated the movements of the head, arms and body. Even though the choreography is hard technically, its timing is so perfect that if you listen to the music Prokofiev almost makes it happen *for* you.

Cinderella's first entrance into the ball is the ultimate rags-to-riches fantasy and is certainly one of my favourite moments. The rags scenes, down in the kitchen, feel quite odd as ballerinas aren't meant to have filthy faces and grubby clothes in the middle of a very classical ballet. (In fact most dancers don't dirt-up their faces as much as they are meant to, because it feels so unnatural.) But in the ball scene I come on in a fabulous gold and silver tutu, making the entrance that not only Cinderella, but every little girl who has ever studied ballet, has dreamed about all her life.

Cinderella enters to some very quiet music, so there's a hush over the whole stage as she *bourrées* on at the back. She seems to float in a trance across the floor as everyone gazes at her. Then, still in a trance, she has to *bourrée* down two flights of steps, being led by the Prince's hand. This is actually quite scary because as Cinderella does this step she's not allowed to look down so she's totally reliant on the man. She just hangs on to him and he squeezes her hand every time she gets to the edge of a stair. I'm always concentrating here on being in perfect time with the music because once I get to the bottom I have to *bourrée* to the front of the stage and then turn immediately around to face everyone. This turn should come on a beautiful musical phrase which almost seems to say, 'Where am I? How magical this is.'

At this moment I *have* to believe in the magic of the fairy tale, so that everyone in the audience can believe too. But you can't force it, you must never gush or grin. I like to imagine Margot here and the kind of aura she projected on stage which forced people to watch her, even though she didn't appear to be trying to seduce them.

By the end of the ballet though I sometimes wish Cinderella didn't have to be so good. It would be satisfying just once to send the Ugly Sisters packing. But then it wouldn't be *Cinderella* and I do always feel unusually happy dancing this ballet. It's not as mentally demanding as a work like *Sleeping Beauty*, for which I really have to psyche myself up. I don't ever feel that *Cinderella* is going to fall apart if I do one thing wrong.

One reason why it feels good dancing so many of Kenneth's ballets, and Sir Fred's, is that the roles have been imagined in so much detail. They make it possible for dancers to get involved with their characters yet also to make the roles their own. In the nineteenth-century classics the choreography is much purer and more academic and every step has to be technically perfect. This obviously gives dancers much less freedom to play with the movement or to find different nuances of expression within it. So in order to make any dramatic sense of a classic role I always have to start out by creating an idea of it in my head. I have to imagine the quality I want to evoke, and let that filter through the steps.

This is especially true in Petipa's *Sleeping Beauty*, which was choreographed in 1890. Even though Aurora is a character who develops from a young girl in Act I to a vision in Act II and finally a woman celebrating her wedding in Act III, the choreography doesn't tell us any detail about what she's feeling as she changes. As the ballerina you are basically having just to smile and look pleasant as you dance.

For instance, in Act I I always want to show that Aurora is quite vulnerable even though she's having a lovely time at her sixteenth birthday party. But Petipa's steps are little more than classroom exercises so they don't communicate any specific emotion – and like most dancers I tend to be distracted from the story line by the fact that my solos are so gruelling to dance. I don't know why this act should be such agony to perform since, step by step, Aurora's solos are quite simple. But during most of the act she is totally exposed at the centre of the stage, and the choreography itself is some of the most physically exhausting in the repertoire. It's very hard to dance classical steps perfectly when you are worn out. In a ballet like *Romeo and Juliet* you can hide behind the drama of the choreography and you don't have to dance every step accurately, but in *Sleeping Beauty* you can't afford to lose the purity of your line for a minute.

In Act II Aurora is a dream figure, being shown off to the Prince by the Lilac Fairy, and it is lovely to dance this straight after Act I when she's been this lively excitable teenager. Suddenly Aurora is much more grown up, but she's also very delicate and fragile. I love the fact that when she's dancing with the Prince he doesn't really support her, his

Swan Lake
© Anthony Crickmay

Aged two, at a friend's birthday party
© *Darcey Bussell*

Preparing for my first ever ballet class at the age of five
© *Darcey Bussell*

My first experience of choreography, aged sixteen, at White Lodge
© Darcey Bussell

With friends in my last year at White Lodge,
when things were looking good
© Darcey Bussell

With Zoltan Solymosi in *Swan Lake*
© *Anthony Crickmay*

With Stuart Cassidy in *The Sleeping Beauty*
© Leslie E Spatt

My 1994 portrait for the National Portrait Gallery by Allen Jones
Allen Jones © National Portrait Gallery

One of the stranger things I've been asked to do – posing with a
De Beers diamond in my mouth for *Tatler*
Neil Kirk © Tatler / The Condé Nast Publications Ltd

My reincarnation as Audrey Hepburn for *Hello*
© John Stoddart

From Kenneth MacMillan's *Elite Syncopations* (ragtime fun)
© *Anthony Crickmay*

The wax version of me
© *Madame Tussauds*

A far cry from the traditional image of a ballerina!

Arthur Elgort © British Vogue / The Condé Nast Publications Ltd

hands just touch her skin. She's very mysterious here, very elusive, but it would make the role even more interesting if Petipa had given Aurora some less obvious steps to dance. She jumps on to the stage doing *jeté, pas de bourrée, jeté, pas de bourrée*, and it's hard to make the choreography look at all otherworldy. I also feel frustrated in Act III when I am trying to show everyone that this is Aurora at her wedding, that she finally has her man and that they are celebrating, but have so little to say it with. The choreography is dramatically very restricted and physically very strenuous, which leaves Aurora trying to look radiant even while her legs are dying.

But despite all its limitations and its terrors I have loved dancing Aurora since I first performed it in 1993, because the ballet possesses such a unique radiance. Even if it lacks dramatic detail, every aspect of the work conspires to make the ballerina feel like a princess: there's so much space on stage, the lighting is so bright and clean, and the role of Aurora has to be danced with such an open, gracious demeanour – Anthony Dowell always says that in *Sleeping Beauty* we have to dance as if we are showing off all our family jewels on our chest.

In *Giselle*, which is an earlier, Romantic ballet, there is more obvious drama than in *Beauty* because the heroine has to change from a peasant girl in Act I to a spirit in Act II. Even so, Giselle has never felt quite real to me as a person. In Act I she's so sweet and naïve and old-fashioned that I feel as if I'm in an old black-and-white movie, while in Act II she's a ghost. The transition between the two acts always seems more radical to me in terms of the choreography, which changes totally. In Act I Giselle's movement is all springing and jumpy, while in Act II she's either drifting like thistledown or sinking her weight deeply into the floor. In Act I she hardly stops dancing, and in Act II she has to remain still for whole passages. Out of all the ballerina roles I've danced (I first performed it in 1995) I find that Giselle has the most helpful costume. The skirt in Act II is so long and light that I really feel as if I'm a spirit, and that I'm being blown by the wind when I do all her little ghostly jumps.

My favourite classic, however, is *Swan Lake*. Obviously the double role of Odette (the White Swan) in Acts II and IV and Odile (the Black Swan) in Act III is a major technical and dramatic challenge, but I also love the fact that there's more freedom to interpret the choreography than in *Sleeping Beauty*. The steps are very classical yet they have a wide range of expression and allow ballerinas to find some personal meaning in the role.

When I was twenty and first started dancing ballerina roles, I didn't fully understand how much dramatic potential they had. I was focusing almost exclusively on the technical hurdles of each ballet, because they were so much harder than anything I'd ever attempted before. But then I started to watch more experienced artists and I realized that technique wasn't the only element that counted in their performance. The Russian ballerina Altynai Asylmuratova, for example, is quite insecure in certain technical areas but her dancing is so expressive – the way she uses her face, her arms and her back – that you don't notice. For Altynai the steps are a way of making us interested in the character that she's dancing, and the music that she's dancing to, rather than an end in themselves.

This is also what Margot Fonteyn taught me when she coached me in *Swan Lake*. She showed me how choreography could be made to tell a story, how a simple *chassée* could become an image of Odette trying to fly away. And I've learnt more from other dancers since then by looking at how different ballerinas portray character, how they project movement, what they accentuate. The Russians, for example, will often accentuate a gesture or a movement in ways that the English would consider vulgar or inappropriate. But it works for them, and it's always fascinating to figure out why.

I used to think that Act III of *Swan Lake* was the hardest of them all because it has the most obvious technical challenges. But the more I've danced the ballet the more I've realized that Act II is the tough one. It isn't the steps which are hard to perfect, but the quality of the movement, which has to look continuous, as if one step were melting into the next.

Most classical dancing involves several parts of the body being co-ordinated at the same time, so that the arms are helping the legs and so on, but in *Swan Lake* you have to move like a huge flying bird. You move your legs, then a split second later your body and then your arms so that there is a constant unfolding of movement. It means that you have to be very strong in the legs and feet, but very soft and curving in the body and arms – and if I've danced the choreography properly my shoulders and back are always in agony the next day. (I have to be careful though, because the movement is so exciting that when I do get it right I feel a huge smile breaking out on my face. I have to remind myself very severely to stay in character.)

The *pas de deux* with Prince Siegfried is totally absorbing however, and I can feel the choreography telling the story for me the whole time. At some moments in the duet Odette is very wary of him still, she is holding herself away from him and ready to fly, but the next minute she's longing for him to take control of the situation again and she sinks against him so that he can wrap his arms around her. The whole *pas de deux* is full of these lovely ebbings and flowings of emotion.

But even when she appears content, Odette is feeling an agony of frustration because she's trapped in the body of a Swan and she knows deep down that the Prince can never break Rothbart's spell and release her. In fact she never stops being terrified of Rothbart; even in Siegfried's arms she can sense his presence and I feel that she's always wanting to look into the back corner to see if he's there, spying on them.

The movement in this duet is dramatically so rich, and Tchaikovsky's music so exquisite that the only thing which prevents me from getting completely carried away is the knowledge that Act III is waiting for me after the interval – with its technically shattering final *pas de deux*.

Some dancers dread the whole of Act III but I find parts of it fabulous to perform – basically because when I first come on stage as Odile I'm feeling like the best thing out there. Even though Odile has to act slightly deferentially to Rothbart and ask him how to manipulate the Prince (they are, after all, partners in crime) she is feeling incredibly powerful. She knows exactly what she wants to do with the Prince, she knows that she has him wrapped around her little finger, and she knows that she is revoltingly gorgeous. It makes such a change to dance a really dangerous woman in the classics – I get tired of having to look pleasant all the time and having to be led by a man.

Then in Act IV I'm back dancing Odette, but by this point in the ballet she feels like a real woman, not a swan at all. She is heartbroken and can't bear to go through anything else; she's lost hope and wants to die. The first part of the act is quite hard to sustain as there is a lot of music but not a lot of action, but then it's always lovely when the Prince comes rushing on stage. There's a thrilling climax in the music which always makes me wish *I* was the Prince at that moment.

I've danced the Kirov version where Odette and the Prince don't actually die at the end. Rothbart gets killed instead and they walk off over him. But I much prefer our version in which we are whisked off to heaven: it's a fabulous visual ending and it feels magical, after all our hard work, to be able to lie close together as we fly off stage, with the Prince lying close to me and protecting me.

Dancing the modern repertoire is of course a brilliant contrast, because not only is the style of movement edgier and more off balance than that of the classics but I'm allowed to be strong as a woman on stage. I don't have to be saved by princes or smile at them sweetly, and in a ballet like Balanchine's *Agon* I am technically as well as dramatically very powerful. My partner and I are physical and sexual equals.

Some of the moves in this ballet are amazing and when I first attempted them in 1991 I thought they were impossible. At one point the woman is holding her leg up in a very high *développé* to the back, and she's keeping her balance by holding on to the man with only one hand. But then, just as she lets go of her leg, he falls to the floor while still hanging on to her and keeping her balanced. Normally if you let go of your foot when it's being held so high the release of tension is almost enough to knock you over. I couldn't believe I had to do this while the man, who was meant to be supporting me, was himself falling to the floor and then rolling over. But I did, and it worked.

Agon doesn't tell a story of any kind but Balanchine built a very intense line of communication between the man and the woman into the choreography. The man and I look at each other nearly the whole time, and even when we don't have eye contact we still have to sense each other's presence through our skin. There's a moment where he comes up to me from behind and we have to catch hands very suddenly – if I wasn't aware of exactly where he was we could never do it fast enough.

What really helped me to understand *Agon* was dancing it with Eddie Shellman when he guested over here from Dance Theatre of Harlem. Eddie is a lovely partner anyway, very sensitive and strong, but he's also black and the ballet was originally choreographed for a white woman (Diana Adams) and a black man (Arthur Mitchell). There's no race issue involved but the visual contrast of colour is crucial. A lot of the choreography has the two dancers wrapping themselves around each other, with one limb crossing over another, and even when the dancers aren't touching there's a very electric sense of closeness, a sense that the air between them is highly charged. I could see all of this so much more clearly when I was dancing with a black partner.

Performing *Agon* in New York was also a revelation. I had a couple of rehearsals with Peter Martins, the director of New York City Ballet, who pointed out a few changes I should make to the steps. But much more important was actually watching the dancers over there. They're trained in Balanchine's style so his special speed and attack come naturally to them, but they also have an energy which is very different from ours. They aren't at all shy or intimidated which means that they have a very direct kind of confidence when they come out on stage. You really need that for dancing Balanchine.

Agon feels like a surprisingly modern work considering that it was created in 1957. But even so, when I dance it I feel that the ballet is well established, that it already has a history and a reputation. When I dance in a brand-new ballet, however, I always feel it has a lot of surprises in store for me, however perfectly I've rehearsed it. It's only after I've performed in public that I feel a role is actually in my body and that I know how an audience will react to it.

When Johnny Cope and I first danced *Pavane* – the duet Christopher Wheeldon created for us in 1997 – we were particularly uncertain about how it would go down. It's technically very scary because a lot of partnerwork relies as much on luck as on judgement. I have to look as though I'm drifting through Johnny's arms in a romantic dream but I'm actually having to work very hard because he's scarcely supporting me at all, and if I fall off balance or something goes wrong, he can't save me.

The ballet is set to a very serene and dreamy score by Ravel – *Pavane pour une Infanta Défunte* – and Chris wanted Johnny and I to dance as though we were moving along a pure line of energy, with nothing speeded up or slowed down. We weren't allowed to jerk or to let it seem that anything was any effort.

During rehearsals Chris explained that we weren't meant to be telling a story but that we *were* meant to look like lovers. He wanted me to imagine myself as Grace Kelly and I understood what he wanted much more clearly when I saw the costumes, which were very 1940s and very stylized. I started to see myself in one of those classic movie scenes where the heroine is drifting off into romantic thoughts about her lover but doesn't for some reason look at him. It's always him that's gazing passionately at her.

This image wasn't always easy to achieve however – particularly in one of the lifts where Johnny had to hold me up high above his shoulders with one hand yet I was only allowed to help him get me up there by pushing off from the ground with one foot. Grace Kelly never had to look romantic wobbling over Cary Grant's head.

Just before the opening show I found myself tensing up badly as I thought of all the things I knew could go wrong, not to mention the things I didn't know about! But Johnny has always had a knack for saying the right thing to calm me down and during the show we pulled off things that we'd had real problems with in rehearsal. The ballet just seemed to come together and it was as if it hadn't quite existed until this moment. When the curtains came down my jaw dropped – I kept saying, 'Oh wow, did you see that? It worked, it worked!'

This was a very important night for Chris as well as for us because it was the first ballet he'd ever made for the Opera House. The buzz from the audience was wonderful, which surprised me slightly because *Pavane* isn't like a gala piece, it doesn't end on a huge climax. The sound of applause was overwhelming and Chris went into a kind of shock. He just wandered around the stage saying over and over again, 'I'm happy . . . I'm very happy . . . I can be happy can't I?'

5

LIFE WITH THE ROYAL BALLET

BALLET DANCERS AREN'T like actors, opera singers or solo musicians who work freelance. We're company creatures who tend to be trained by a company school, rise up through company ranks and probably stay with that company for most of our performing lives.

Of course there are famous exceptions, like Igor Zelensky or Sylvie Guillem, who choose to cut loose from their roots and perform with many different companies around the world, and of course there are advantages to that style of career. Freelance dancers can demand high fees and have an enviable amount of power: they can dictate the terms of their contracts, they can choose their partners, and they don't have to comply with company rules.

But it's not a life that would suit me – at least right now – because I feed off the other dancers around me. I depend on knowing people well in class and on stage, not only for emotional support but to make the work fun. There is so much pressure on me as a principal that if I had no friends in the company it would be hard to bear. It would make my working life rather unreal.

In fact being on friendly terms with other dancers can affect even the smallest things. If my character has to be in conversation with other characters during a performance I need to have a genuine rapport with those dancers otherwise our acting would look stilted and artificial. If I'm dancing a very demanding role, like Aurora, it helps to feel that the rest of the stage is on my side. It would be alienating to operate as a guest artist all the time. At The Royal, when outsiders come in to perform we basically just want to be impressed by them – we want them to be technical wizards, we don't care so much what they're like as people.

Still, compared to some other companies I've guested with The Royal is quite relaxed and amicable. It's important to most of us to maintain good relations even with people we don't particularly like, and we are conscious that we have to look good together on stage so we respect each other's work and give each other support.

But of course we aren't angels – we all have sensitive egos and the nature of our profession makes us highly competitive. When I come back to work after our long summer break it's one of the things I always notice and dislike most. After weeks of relaxing, we get back into the studio and we're immediately sizing each other up – checking out who's lost weight and who's gained it, who's looking in shape and who isn't. If I spot someone who's obviously been taking class all through the holiday instead of having a break I will be thinking, 'Idiot, they'll fizzle out half way through the season because they haven't had a rest.' But actually I'm jealous because they're looking better than I am.

And of course that competitive undercurrent never goes away. It's often most obvious in daily class where we're all striving to improve our technique. As we try to perform more turns or hold our balances for longer we're pitting ourselves against each other. We're also trying to get ourselves noticed by our teachers because competition is always very fierce when it comes to being chosen for roles and getting promoted within the company. Some dancers may complain that they are being too severely criticized in class, even that their teachers are bullying them, but it means they are being noticed.

Ultimately Anthony, as director, casts all the ballets so even when new choreographers come into the company he recommends suitable dancers to them. The principals and some of the soloists are fortunate because they are sent cast lists privately, a couple of weeks before the rest of the company – they don't have to let anyone see their disappointment or their pleasure. But everyone else has to wait until the cast lists are pinned up on the notice-boards. Casting decisions are made about six months in advance and it's always like waiting for exam results when they come out. Everyone is praying that they will have been moved up a line in the *corps de ballet* or will have got the solo role they've been hoping for.

As a principal I'm lucky enough to know that I will be doing at least one performance of each classic, but I may still be tense about which first nights I'll be given. Some ballets, like *Giselle*, I never expect to dance in the opening show because it's not a role that I'm considered particularly suited to, but if there are some good revivals coming up during the season then it matters a lot to me that I'll get an opportunity to dance them early on.

We passionately want to be chosen for new ballets or new productions, and the claws certainly come out over the first cast for these. Three different dancers may have been chosen to learn each of the leading roles but the choreographer often doesn't decide until quite late who will be first cast. So rehearsals can become very edgy. Several dancers may be doing the same solo in the studio together and it's not uncommon for one of them to start doing the steps slightly ahead of the others so that they are noticed first by the choreographer, or for one to crowd the others out so they don't have space to dance properly.

It sounds demeaning but it's surprisingly easy to fall into that kind of behaviour because managing our competitive instincts is hard. I know that I'm very competitive myself, and since it's a quality that I dislike I try not to be too obvious about it. But I also know that I wouldn't have got anywhere in my career without it.

Like any dancer I am highly critical of myself and I have to be a ruthless perfectionist, but that inevitably makes me critical of everyone else's work. When I'm watching other dancers I will automatically be looking out for their good and bad points and I'll probably compare notes with anyone else who's watching. It's all too easy for those kinds of conversations to slide from the analytic ('if she did this it would look better than if she did that') to the bitchy. And bitchy remarks always get back. I wish as a company we were better at giving each other compliments. We may talk about how good someone's show has been behind their back but we rarely say it directly to their face, and this is ridiculous because compliments from fellow dancers are always the best. If someone tells me that I've done a good show I'm flattered as I know that the dancer has seen me working every day and isn't easy to impress. So I do try to make a point of being positive to other dancers. But we can't be too nice because it's the rivalry between us that keeps us hungry and drives our careers. We need the knife edge of competition to keep us striving for new and better roles and to stop us from becoming complacent about our techniques. The bottom line is also that we don't want anyone else to be too good because we don't want anyone standing in the way of our own chance of promotion.

For some dancers, promotion can take years to come their way. They may be very talented in class but for some reason they don't catch the management's eye, or else they may have become typecast doing certain solo roles and haven't been given the chance to attempt principal ones. There is favouritism in any company and obviously the management has a certain taste in dancers, which can work against some people.

Some dancers are also much better in performance than they are in studio and they have to wait for a lucky break to get them out on stage. They may, unfortunately, have to pray for someone else to get injured. If they turn out to be quick learners and can not only pick up a role fast but cope with performing at the last minute, they will always do well in the end. For any company, getting a show on stage is the bottom line – so quick, reliable dancers are precious.

I know how lucky I was to be promoted from *corps* to soloist so fast and not to have to go through that agonizing first stage of wondering whether anyone would notice me. I was lucky too to be earning a principal's salary so young. It begins at around a basic £30,000 and is then negotiable upwards, and it was a huge jump for me from the meagre pay of a *corps de ballet* artist. But I did put a lot of people's noses out of joint by rising so rapidly. There were several older dancers in the company who felt they had been unfairly passed over when they saw me being appointed over their heads, and there were a lot of comments along the lines that I would have been a better, and more deserving principal if I had danced in the *corps* for a couple more years.

Even as a principal though, the competition doesn't ease off. There are always talented dancers coming up through the company behind me, and being at the top I am more vulnerable to criticism. If I make even a small mistake it gets noticed, and some people are quick to put me down for it.

Certainly as far as the management are concerned we are only as good as our last show. I sometimes feel that while I have been working very reliably and consistently more erratic dancers get noticed because they've suddenly pulled off a great performance. I also know that the public and the critics want variety – they like to see new faces – and the company itself has an obligation to promote all of its talent. So even though my position at The Royal may seem very strong I am never allowed to feel safe. And of course I am constantly, and not always favourably, compared to Sylvie Guillem – at least by the press.

Ever since I was made a principal, journalists have fantasized about us being deadly rivals. They would love to think that we scratch each other's eyes out every time we meet in the corridors of the Opera House. In fact we're rarely in direct competition as we don't perform together much on the same stage. Ballet isn't like a tennis match. And even though we're not close friends – Sylvie has chosen not to get very involved with the company – we are always perfectly pleasant to each other. But she is such an extraordinary dancer that I can't help comparing myself with her. I envy her her body, and its amazing technical ease, and I do need to prove to myself that I can do all the things that she's capable of. I'm aware too that she projects a confidence on stage that I don't possess and I have to admit that her presence in The Royal makes some things awkward for me.

As a guest artist with the company, Sylvie dances about fifteen shows a year and is given a lot of choice about what dates she performs. If I want to organize guest appearances with other companies I always have to fit my diary around her dates, which is naturally frustrating. Sylvie also gets first choice of partner – which is nearly always Johnny – and I mind about that too. I love dancing with Johnny and sometimes I'm left performing with a partner who is not nearly so well suited to me, or who doesn't know the ballet so well. So there have been occasions when I've felt angry that my own performances have suffered due to Sylvie taking precedence.

But the benefits of having her in the company outweigh the problems. When she first joined she was a challenge to everyone – we'd never seen a dancer with a body like hers – and she inspired people to raise their technical ambitions. As for me, whenever people assume that Sylvie must have taken certain roles away from me I say, 'No, Sylvie's actually given me roles.' Because the wonderful thing about Sylvie is that she is tall, the same height as me.

British dancers are generally much shorter than the Americans, Russians or French so at five foot seven (and over six foot on point) I've always been a bit of an oddity here. (I love guesting abroad because suddenly I'm not towering over everyone else. In a gala I once appeared with four other ballerinas dancing the Rose Adage together – and for the first time in my life I was the smallest woman on stage.) There's also always been an assumption in The Royal that certain roles such as Giselle and Juliet can only be performed by small dancers. But of course when Sylvie joined, audiences wanted to see her in all the big classics so she danced those roles as a matter of course. And she proved that being tall isn't a limitation. With the right partner, any dancer can act as though she is young and vulnerable, any dancer can endear herself to an audience.

So Sylvie broke an important barrier for me, and when I started dancing principal roles being tall was far less of an issue than it would have been a decade earlier. Even so, my height has always felt a sensitive point; I'm not everyone's idea of a ballerina, and I've never been able to decide whether that's a good or a bad thing.

Obviously it helped a lot when Kenneth insisted that one reason why he needed me for *Pagodas* was that he loved my height and strength. He used to say that The Royal was too obsessed with finding another ballerina in the same mould as Margot, and that I was a very modern dancer with a very modern scale and attack.

My height has always brought me attention from the press, but certain journalists have used it against me, particularly when I've had problems finding partners who were tall enough for me. Reading some articles it sounds as though I've run through hundreds of men and that I'm a nightmare to cast. Of course with Sylvie having first claim on Johnny there have been occasions when it's been hard finding partners; sometimes we've had to look outside the company – both Zoltan Solymosi and Robert Hill were partly (though not entirely) hired because they were tall enough for me. I have also since discovered Igor (Zelensky) who I love to dance with. But I've had some experiences when I've thought I would be stuck without any partner at all.

I remember one matinée show of *Swan Lake* when no one seemed available. I'd originally been cast with Adam Cooper but he'd injured himself and couldn't dance. Johnny was out of the question because he was dancing the evening show with Sylvie, and though I'm often partnered by Cassidy I needed someone with more height for a romantic ballet like *Swan Lake*. The only other tall principal, William Trevitt, was also injured and by this time Zoltan and Robert had both left the company.

In desperation I finally suggested that we tried out one of the *corps de ballet*, an Argentinian called Inaki Urlezaga who's a lovely guy and a very good dancer. He'd already done some partnering in a couple of ballets and as it was a matinée show I thought it would be a safe moment to try him out. In the end it turned out that I fell ill too and was unable to perform the show, but it was a good break for Inaki. He's gone on to do quite a lot of principal roles and we've danced together several times since.

As a child my height didn't make me particularly self-conscious, in fact I didn't really grow tall until I reached the Upper School and by then I was determined to make it work to my advantage. The fact that no one could miss me meant I had to dance my best the whole time and could never fade into anonymity during class. But I began to feel awkward in *pas de deux* classes, where I towered over some of the boys. Even with some of the taller ones I'd find that when I was balancing with them on point I was the wrong size for resting my cheek against theirs, or forming the correct classical line. It's in *pas de deux* still that I sometimes get depressed about my height. There are many lifts which can look so lovely and effortless with a tiny ballerina like Viviana Durante. Small women are easy to pick up, whereas I, being tall and strong, weigh a lot more and am more difficult to throw around.

I remember when we were making *Pavane* that I got particularly upset about my size. It was still quite close to the beginning of the season and I wasn't properly back in shape after the holidays so I became very self-conscious about being lifted during rehearsals. Johnny has never complained about lifting me and always thinks that I'm ridiculous to worry. He says: 'Have I ever said anything about your weight? No, so just shut up about it.' He even insists that it's easier partnering me than small women because he doesn't have to bend down to lift me – I'm a good height for him. But I couldn't help believing that with someone smaller in my role Chris Wheeldon could have done so many more interesting things – despite the fact that Chris himself insisted that he'd picked me because I looked so much more impressive.

Unfortunately the public tend to think of ballerinas being delicate rather than impressive so I have to be tough with myself and think, 'Yes, I could struggle and lose a stone, but there are more important things in the world than whether I look beautiful in a lift.' And I have to hold on to the fact that I have qualities which smaller dancers don't possess. I know that my movements look cleaner and clearer because I'm tall, that I can travel a long way through space and that I'm fast.

Still, my insecurities are always close to the surface and the time I was pulled out of *Manon* they boiled over. The combination of circumstances – the management not explaining their motives clearly and the press making such a meal of the story – left me feeling as if I'd been given a huge and humiliating slap around the face. I was so upset that I went into the whole spoiled ballerina routine and refused to go to work for a week. People tried to reason with me by saying I was at the beginning of my career and should be able to handle a setback, but it was precisely because I *was* at the beginning of my career that the situation shook my confidence badly.

But I went back to work because, like any dancer, if I'm going to perform with a company then I have to live with company politics. I can't just see everything from my own point of view because we're dependent on each other if we want to put on a good show. We all have to survive the pressure together.

The pressures which affect a ballet company are often not well understood by the public and the press; at The Royal we have such a large repertoire and present so many programmes during a single season that the work load can be very intense. We often go on stage feeling badly prepared for a ballet either because we've lost rehearsal time through some of the dancers being taken off to work on other productions, or because there haven't been enough studios or coaches available to get us ready for our individual roles. I remember when we revived *Pagodas* I was terribly frustrated at how little time was being spent on getting the ballet ready and how convinced I was that it would look shoddy on stage. For some reason *Pagodas* hadn't been the main focus of that season's rehearsal schedule, despite the fact that it has a large cast and many dancers performing in the revival hadn't even seen the ballet, let alone danced in it. Basically, most of the new cast had no idea what they were doing. Monica Parker (the ballet's notator), who was taking rehearsals, was shocked when she realized that the *corps* needed teaching from scratch. And because she couldn't get into every rehearsal Johnny and I had to teach a lot of the choreography to the other new principals.

During rehearsals we'd also been held up by arguments over the choreography. When the ballet was filmed for television and video Kenneth had made some changes to the steps which had never been recorded in the notation. I remembered these when we came to revive the ballet, but though the ballet master and the notator had seen the film they wanted to stick with the notated version. It all became rather fraught. I felt that Kenneth's last intentions should be honoured, but of course everyone has their own ideas about staging ballets.

Irek and I had some fierce disagreements when we came to revive *Winter Dreams* too, and again this was after Kenneth's death so he wasn't there to settle them. We each wanted to do lifts differently and we each remembered phrases differently, so we kept having to go and check the notator's score to see who was right.

When I danced in Ashton's *Cinderella* in 1996 the

arguments over steps were even more complicated because some of the dancers had discovered a film of a 1968 performance of the ballet in which Ashton and Robert Helpmann were dancing the Ugly Sisters and Anthony Dowell and Antoinette Sibley were dancing the principal roles. They got very excited when they saw how much of the choreography had altered since that film and there was a lot of debate about which version we should dance. One camp wanted to return to the film version while the other thought we should stick to the one that was staged ten years previously for Johnny and Maria Almeida when Ashton was still alive. Ashton had actually updated the ballet slightly then and we had a video of that production.

Wendy Ellis was also in the studio coaching, and she had her own views about the revival as well. Wendy is the widow of the late Michael Somes – who used to coach all the Ashton repertoire – and she danced in the ballet herself during the '70s and '80s. So I was often left standing in the middle of rehearsals while all these people argued over how I should be dancing.

These kinds of delays are frustrating when rehearsal time is already so pressured. There are some busy periods, when I'm dancing several different roles, during which I feel that I'm simply churning out ballets. I get badly depressed because I don't have time to perfect anything or to bring anything fresh to a role. One season was so hectic that I danced my first performance of Nikiya in *La Bayadère* without anyone having coached me in the mime scenes.

It's also difficult when we're swapping between very

different styles of ballet during a single day's rehearsals. It's quite easy to go from one classic to another as all the choreography has the same technical base, but it can be a jolt switching from a very modern ballet like a Tharp or a Forsythe back to a work like *Sleeping Beauty*. And I do need to rehearse the classics well, even if I've danced them dozens of times before. I need the reassurance of going through a role thoroughly at least three times before I open, to make sure I'm confident in it.

But I don't always manage it, and I do yearn for the kind of intensive coaching I used to receive as a new principal when I was first dancing the classics. Anthony and Antoinette (Sibley) always give individual coaching to dancers who are new to a role so that their first night is very special. The problem is, we all still crave that kind of attention. I'm always hungry to improve, I always feel that there's so much in my roles that I'm not yet achieving, but as a senior principal I can't demand that kind of nurturing.

It comes as a shock to me actually to realize how senior I now am. When I was first rehearsing with Inaki in *Swan Lake* he kept saying how grateful and happy he was to be dancing with someone as high up in the company as me – though most of the time I feel as if I'm still nineteen and just starting out. And I notice a similar deference among some of the most junior dancers too, which makes me uncomfortable because I feel as though I'm getting cut off from the rest of the company. Some of the newest *corps* members don't dare talk to me at first even though I still change in the *corps de ballet* dressing room at Baron's Court. If I'm in there and a couple of new girls walk in I might say something ordinary to them like 'Gosh, what a hard rehearsal. Don't your feet feel awful?' and for a moment they just stare at me and I can see them thinking, 'Darcey Bussell's just asked me how my feet are!'

Part of the problem is that I don't rehearse with many dancers any more except during full company rehearsals. Usually I'm being coached alone or with a partner, and when we do all come together I'm having to concentrate so hard on my own role that there's not much time to relax and chat. But I hate to think I'll ever be treated like a guest artist or some unapproachable diva because when people behave as if I'm an awesome prima ballerina I feel ridiculous.

I had one very unnerving experience of this when I attended a gala performed by the National Youth Ballet at the Opera House. I'm their patron and I'd agreed to present an award after the show, but when I came on stage these very young dancers crowded round and just stared at me. I tried talking to them about how well the show had gone and how hard it must have been for them as they'd had so little rehearsal on the stage, but they couldn't speak to me. They just whispered to each other, 'It's Darcey Bussell, it's Darcey Bussell, it's Darcey Bussell.'

The same thing happens when pupils from White Lodge come in and work with the company. If I pass them in a corridor I hear them whispering in little groups, 'Darcey Bussell Darcey Bussell Darcey Bussell.' I suppose I feel honoured, but it makes me self-conscious too. They're watching every move I make and I begin to watch myself too. I start feeling that I have to behave very properly and set a good example.

All the same I don't think that ballerinas are regarded with the kind of reverence they used to be, and this is a recent change. When I first arrived in the company younger dancers would never speak to a principal unless they were spoken to first. But now, once dancers have got used to being in the company, they tend to develop a much more confident attitude. Someone quite young and cocky will feel perfectly relaxed about standing in front of me in class and won't care that I'm her senior. She's out to make her own way in the world. If I want her respect I have to earn it.

Some ballet fans may feel nostalgia for the magical aura that used to surround ballerinas like Fonteyn, but companies develop a much more supportive attitude without it. When I'm on stage I feel that the other dancers are behind me, and that if I make a mistake the *corps* will be willing me to recover. I can hear them whispering to me: 'Come on, Darce, come on.' We'd never have done that to a ballerina when I was first in the company, but we *would* all have been whispering together, 'Ooh, did you see *her* slip.'

That kind of bitchy distance is horrible for senior principals to deal with. We all need the support of other dancers when things are going badly for us, and one of the times that we need it most is when we are injured. It's when I've been injured that I've been most thankful that I work in a company, because that is usually the most vulnerable point in any dancer's career.

*

These days injury is likely to affect all of us, for ballet has become so intensively athletic that our bodies inevitably pay the price in some way. If we never injured ourselves, it would actually mean that we weren't pushing ourselves hard enough and were being too precious in our dancing.

Some of the injuries I've suffered are, I'm sure, the result of having pushed myself so hard at every challenge when I was young. As I struggled to make myself perfect in the big ballerina roles, I didn't worry about the effect it was having on my body. I was so determined not to have any limitations, I was so determined to do every step that was given me. Now I've learnt more about how to service my body, how to warm it up properly and how to pace myself. So even though I might sometimes get overexcited about my work and forget to take care about landing properly out of a jump or to take enough rest, I don't abuse my body so badly. I think and hope that my injuries are fizzling out now.

Whenever I *have* been injured I've always found it irksome that the press latch on to the fact so quickly. Even if I miss only a couple of shows journalists start speculating about whether I'm suffering from burn-out or whether I'm not looking after myself. There are usually several other dancers injured at the same time but no one writes about them, and the press rarely mention *why* or *how* I've become injured, when it can have been someone else's fault entirely.

For example, about three years ago I had a bad fall which was caused by slipping on a loose floor cloth. It happened during a stage call for *Manon*, which had started late due to the stage crew having had some problems with moving the props. The crew had had to put the floor cloth (which covers the stage) down quickly to save time and no one noticed that there was a gap in the old wooden surface underneath. So during my first *pas de deux*, at the point where Des Grieux has to slide Manon across the floor, my foot caught in the gap. The cloth gathered up and held it fast, while my partner Zoltan was still trying to push me along. My foot buckled right over, straining the tendons, and I burst into tears. The pain was agonizing but far worse was the feeling of black panic I felt at the possibility of being seriously injured. This was at a time when I'd only recently recovered from surgery on a damaged foot, and I knew the press would start their endless querying about my health even though the fall hadn't been my fault. Luckily it wasn't my bad foot which had got caught, but I was still off work for a couple of months.

Dancers are always so desperate not to miss any part of their careers that we find it tempting to work through injuries if we possibly can. When we first join the company we're especially determined to prove ourselves, and I know many dancers who have been injured but who have carried on working without telling anyone. It's dangerous and self-defeating because the body develops bad scar tissue if it's made to work while injured, and it may never heal properly. Other problems may also develop as the body tries to protect itself, which can flare up later on and prove incurable.

So we know that we should be sensible and cautious but even so I will often work through a minor injury like a muscle strain, not only because I can't bear to miss a show but because I have such a stubborn pride about not being a wimp. I've done more performances than I like to remember with hot packs strapped to my back in order to prevent a damaged muscle going into spasm, and every time, afterwards, I cannot believe I've taken such a stupid risk.

I've even attempted to dance *Sleeping Beauty* with a raging fever – and had to be brought off after Act I. The show was just after Christmas in 1996 and I knew that I'd been going down with flu for several days. But I'd never missed a performance through illness before so I hoped that if I drugged myself up with Nurofen and slept for most of the afternoon I would get through the show.

Two hours before opening I could hardly speak but I took my temperature and it was, if anything, lower than normal. So I thought I was all right to go on stage. However, by the time I got to dancing the Rose Adage I felt totally unreal, my legs had gone numb, I had no energy and I felt so dizzy I could barely spot during any of my pirouettes. When I came off stage I was ready to collapse and let my cover, Belinda Hatley, take over. But unfortunately Belinda had been told to go back to her dressing room as I had seemed to be managing, so I had to finish the act. By the time it was over I was burning with fever and couldn't possibly dance another step. But this was one of those frustrating occasions when everyone watching said that it was one of the best Rose Adages I'd ever performed. The fact that I was simply trying to stay on my feet meant that I couldn't worry about any of the steps or wind myself up in my usual fashion. I just looked wonderfully relaxed.

After that show I was in bed for over a week and missed several performances. People might think a dancer would be grateful for the rest but we are all obsessives. Even though I love to take a break when I'm on holiday, I feel only half alive if I'm not able to dance during the season. So the six months in 1994 when I was off work having foot surgery was one of the bleakest and most testing times I've ever experienced.

The surgery was to remove a bone spur at the base of my right ankle which had probably started developing when I sprained my ankle at the age of twelve. The doctors assumed I must have chipped off a tiny piece of bone which had then calcified into a spur. This had grown so large it was rubbing against my tendons and restricting my movement so, for instance, whenever I tried to bend my ankle into a *plié* I couldn't go down as deeply as I needed.

For dancers, surgery is always the last option when dealing with injury because it is so traumatic. We can rarely be certain that it will solve the problem and the body takes a long time to recover. So even though the doctors confirmed that the spur wouldn't go away without an operation, I was determined to put it off for as long as I could. It was the beginning of the season, and it was a specially good one for me – I had *Romeo and Juliet* and a new production of *Sleeping Beauty* coming up – so I trailed around several specialists to find out whether they thought I could continue dancing for a few more months, and opted to try and get through the season with a cortizone injection.

The cortizone would cushion the spur and reduce the inflammation in the surrounding tissue but no one could promise how long its effect would last, or even if it would work at all. So I just had to cross my fingers and go for it, not realizing how excruciating it would be. The needle was huge and the doctor had to prod all around the inflamed area to make sure the cortizone had spread everywhere it was needed. When I stood up I nearly fainted – just at the moment that the doctor was telling me I could take class again in three days!

The next day my foot felt so stiff I thought it had been a failure. But as the doctor predicted, I was dancing after three days and the cortizone did its work for nearly the whole season. The body hates to be meddled with, though, it always makes you pay, and gradually I realized it was beginning to do some very odd things to protect itself. I began to *plié* in a strange fashion, rolling my foot and ankle forward from the injured part, and the whole right side of my back grew stiffer while my pelvis moved slightly. I also began to get a pain on the inside of my foot which turned out to be the beginnings of a stress fracture caused by the way it was compensating for the spur.

But I'm very very stubborn and I managed to perform both *Romeo and Juliet* and the first night of *Sleeping Beauty* in Washington, and to get as far as the stage calls for *Don Quixote*. I was determined to dance the role of Kitri in that ballet as I'd never performed it before, and I was also determined to go on tour with the company to New York – I'd been given such a lovely reception there when I'd guested with New York City Ballet. But my body was getting increasingly uncooperative and at one of the general calls for

Don Quixote – very close to the opening night – my foot and ankle began to hurt badly. I went back to the doctor and pleaded for another cortizone injection but he said that if I danced any more on the spur I could do serious long-term damage.

So I had to give in. At the beginning of June I cancelled the *Don Quixote* performances and in July, when everyone else went off to New York, I went into hospital.

Having made the decision to go ahead with surgery I didn't initially feel too bad. I'd had a long time to prepare myself emotionally, and I'd got so sick of my bad foot and so bored of having to be careful with it that I was desperate to get the bone spur out of the way. I had no idea, though, how physically disabled I would be, and how much I would hate feeling that way.

When I came round from the anaesthetic the doctors tried to get me standing on my foot immediately. I tried to comply – a ballerina can always get up on her feet – but as soon as my bad foot touched the floor I felt such a huge rush of blood to it that my stomach churned and I fell straight back on to the bed.

I felt so pathetic having a body that didn't work any more, and so scared, because I've always needed to feel that I'm in control. Suddenly, rather than aspiring to turn thirty-two double *fouettés*, the limit of my ambition was tottering down the hospital corridor and back. But during my week in hospital I was given physiotherapy every day so at least I felt I was taking my first steps back to recovery. And it was probably fortunate that I didn't know how long that recovery would take – or I might have been tempted to give up.

When I was allowed home my foot was braced in a kind of bionic boot, which was torture. I had to sit with my foot sticking up in the air, and when I hobbled around I had to be careful about every step. I wasn't allowed to use crutches in case they made me walk crookedly and put my spine out of alignment, and when I went up and down stairs I had to haul myself up each step using the banister. I was longing to swim and to get my body moving again, but for six weeks I wasn't allowed to get my scar wet.

As well as having to cope with all my frustrated energy, I had to come to terms with my bizarre appearance. My bad ankle had ballooned so drastically that it wasn't an ankle any more while the calf muscles had virtually wasted away from disuse. My legs looked as if they belonged to two completely different people.

It had never crossed my mind what a strain this period would be, and one of the few things that saved me was the fact that six other dancers in the company were also injured. Two of them were recovering from operations, and when I started to go into work for physio and massage we could compare notes and feel sorry for ourselves together.

By the beginning of August I was well enough to go on holiday and Angus and I headed for the sun and sea. It was such a physical relief to swim every day and to watch the salt water and sun healing my scar, and I began to think that I was making excellent progress. When I returned home I did two weeks of Pilates training, to begin toning up my muscles and prepare my foot, and I also had some intensive sessions with the sports psychologist at The Royal who helped me adjust myself mentally to the idea of going back to work.

I hadn't realized how badly the mind as well as the body is scarred after injury, nor how deeply our thoughts influence us as dancers. At this point I still had some very bad memories of how painful it had been to make certain movements and at one level I was terrified of trying them again. Obviously this was going to have a very inhibiting effect on my dancing so during therapy I learnt how to focus on all these negative thoughts and block them out, then visualize my way through an entire class trying to re-experience the sensation of dancing without injury. I even learnt how to visualize all the blood in my veins and feel it pumping through my foot, to heal the wound. I began these sessions as a complete sceptic but I was rapidly converted. Whenever I concentrated on visualizing the blood in my foot I could actually feel it getting hotter!

I began to believe that I might soon be dancing again, and just before the season started I took my first class, with Betty Anderton. The other dancers were lovely and welcoming, saying, 'Oh Darcey, how amazing, you're back already,' and I was feeling very proud of myself and predicting that I'd be back doing shows soon. But almost immediately my foot and ankle began to give me trouble again. I thought it was just post-operation stiffness, something I had to work through, and that it would be fine if I did only simple exercises at the barre. So for a few days I ignored the pain and pushed myself a little bit harder every class. But then the inside of my foot became badly inflamed, and I could barely work it.

I felt distraught. This was worse than being back to square one as I couldn't even take a class. Fortunately Monica (Mason) is a genius at coping with injured dancers and after a couple of sessions, during which she analysed minutely what I was doing with my feet, she diagnosed the problem. Essentially my bad foot was behaving as if the bone spur was still there and was putting itself under stress to compensate for a problem that didn't exist any more. It's amazing how the body learns to take the most comfortable route through work and how unwilling it is to unlearn bad habits.

So I virtually had to learn how to dance again from scratch. During some sessions I spent thirty minutes simply pointing and flexing my feet, and on good days I'd be allowed to do half a pirouette at the barre. It was hideously frustrating because I had to take everything so slowly – if I slightly overworked my body one day I had to ease up the next. Even though I seemed to be crawling along Monica insisted that I was absolutely truthful with her and told her whenever my foot hurt. I became obsessed with my own pain, I think it drove me a little bit mad having to focus on it every day.

Even when I started to do more steps I still didn't feel that I was making progress because the way I danced had become very uneven. I still couldn't *plié* properly on one side, and when I jumped I couldn't point my bad foot in the air nor did I have any real power in my bad leg to push off from the ground. I'd always had a natural jump, now I felt like a bird with a damaged wing, hopping around and unable to fly.

After about two months with Monica I was finally allowed to go back and do company class twice a week, and I was in heaven dancing to music again. But I was horrified at how fast the class seemed to be whizzing along. Although I could now do all the steps I could only manage them at half the speed. I felt like a convalescent.

It was painful having everyone in the company see me dance so badly so I hid in a corner and tried to concentrate on myself. People would ask how I was and I wouldn't admit how miserable and vulnerable I felt. I'd be breezy and cheery and say I was fine and coming on very well and was sure I'd be back soon. But there was no way I could perform any of the shows which had originally been scheduled for me, nor would I be able to dance Aurora when the company filmed our new production of *Sleeping Beauty* for television. Even though it comforted me to know that I had been Anthony's first choice for the film it hurt badly to miss it.

However, my greatest concern was that the longer I remained off work the more I began to panic about returning. Even though my foot was finally working properly again, I was badly out of shape, I had very little stamina and I was feeling chronic stage fright.

For a principal it is distressingly hard getting back to performing as we can't ease ourselves in gently by doing a few shows in the back row of the *corps*. To dance a principal role we have to be nearly one hundred per cent back on form. I begged Monica to let me do a couple of *corps de ballet* shows in secret, or one of the Big Swan solos, just to get over my stage fright, but she said there was no point. Instead we spent about a fortnight working on sections of solos together, with Monica always allowing me to change the choreography if a step was difficult. So, painfully, I got my body and my confidence back together until she thought I was ready to go on stage.

My first role was only a short one, Ashton's *Raymonda pas de deux*, and I managed to get through it competently enough after my six months of absence. Unfortunately though, when I looked at the pictures taken of me afterwards, I felt that no one should have let me near a stage. Because to my own eyes at least, I looked huge.

I hadn't weighed myself during this period but I suppose I must have known that I was about six or seven pounds heavier than my usual eight and a half stone. After all, I hadn't been working my body as hard as normal and I'd been deliberately eating well to speed up the healing process. You can't diet if you want your body to mend. Even so, I hadn't realized how big an extra half-stone would make me feel and this was yet another blow to my confidence.

Even four months later I was still feeling low about my dancing and extremely nervous about the fact that I was scheduled to appear in a gala in Canada. As soon as I walked into the first rehearsal for the event I knew that my coming was a terrible mistake. There were dancers from all over the world, the best of the best, and I was totally unprepared to be seen on the same stage. But at least one very good thing came out of it. I was feeling so tentative that I slipped during that first rehearsal and went right over on my bad foot. A bolt of pain flashed through it and I thought, 'That's it, I've wrecked my foot again.' But actually the pain turned out to be the ripping of some post-surgery scar tissue, which had been bothering me for months. The scar had stiffened and was preventing me from stretching my foot properly. Suddenly I could move it easily again and it felt like a sign that everything would finally be OK.

Even though that whole period was so bleak to live through, I did come away with some positive results too. While I was being forced to go back to basics with my dancing I learned some essential lessons about how my body works and about the way I dance which I would never have discovered any other way. More importantly, the injury itself forced me to re-think the way I approached ballet as an art form. I realized that I couldn't always count on my body to impress, and that I should concentrate more on the way I expressed myself. I began to see how I could prepare for roles in my mind as well as in my body. So although I'd never wish the experience on anyone else, it did give me a new view of my art, and certainly made me a better dancer.

Now, whenever I know that a younger dancer has been in-jured, I try to sympathize with her depression and to convince her that some good can come of it. Though it's hard to believe, dancers can make twice as much progress while they're not performing as they can when they are fulfilling their normal workload, simply because that's the only time they ever get to focus exclusively on themselves.

But stoical as I learned to be I never stopped regretting that I missed out on the company trip to New York, because touring abroad is always one of the most exciting parts of the season.

Travelling is a passion for me and I love the fact that performing with the company can take me to countries like Japan, China or Argentina which I'd probably never visit on holiday. I also enjoy the way that being on tour brings us closer as a company, because of all the time we spend together, and some of the adventures we have.

On the other hand, travelling with a hundred and twenty people can be extremely tedious as the whole company has to arrive at the airport about three hours early, then hang around while they are checked off lists and sorted into groups. Organizing our lives and our luggage for an eight-week tour is also a logistical nightmare. We have to pack for all the climatic eventualities of the tour so that we don't boil or freeze, and if we are going to countries with very different cultures (and different shops) we have to remember all the little extras that we can't live without. Dancers' tour boxes are filled with the oddest things like packets of soup, plasters and Nurofen. We also never travel without our bible – the Red Touring Book – which contains everything we need to know about travel arrangements and about the countries we're visiting, from currency and bank times to restaurant hours, local customs and the names and numbers of Embassies if ever we get into trouble.

When we're travelling long distances, jet lag is obviously a problem. The principals who are dancing on the opening night usually arrive a day or two early to give them time to acclimatize, but even so the worst moment of a tour is arriving at a studio to begin rehearsals and feeling as if we are still on a plane, or that we should still be fast asleep. Most dancers need boringly routine lives to perform at their best. Our bodies don't like irregular sleep patterns and changes in time zones. And for us in The Royal it's always a shock having to dance eight shows in a row as we often do on tour, since at home in Covent Garden we alternate performances with the Opera.

At home too we have the right size rehearsal studios and a familiar stage. On tour I've had to rehearse in one studio that was only big enough for a couple of children to skip around in and in another where the ceiling was so low we hit our heads every time we jumped. In Buenos Aires when our stage wasn't ready for us we had to take company class in a boxing ring, with the air full of the smell of stale popcorn from the previous night's match. And in the same city we've had a crucial stage call cancelled because the lighting crew had gone on strike and wouldn't come back until the theatre had paid their wages.

These things are obviously a strain, but they also take the pressure off us dancers because it becomes such an adventure just getting the show on stage. At the best of times there is an old-fashioned romance about touring which I remember feeling very vividly when we danced in Israel.

We were performing *Swan Lake* in an outdoor arena and the temperature was so hot that we couldn't take class till five o'clock in the afternoon or begin the performance until the sun had gone down. The *corps* were in bliss, sitting on the beach or by the pool all afternoon but I had to stay inside because the sunshine is so draining I would never have made it through three acts of Odette/Odile if I'd been out all day tanning myself. (Contrary to popular opinion dancers *are* allowed to get tanned, even if they have to become swans in the evening, because our body make-up (wet-white) can easily cover up the brown. Burning though is forbidden. Red skin turns a very weird shade of purple under the wet-white and it chafes agonizingly under the shoulder straps of our tutus.)

Even by evening, Israel was still hot and humid and during the show all our point shoes started to melt. I had to change mine twice during each act because I kept finding that I was dancing on soggy mush. We were also sweating pints – it was dripping down from under my headdress and my partner and I got so slippery we could hardly feel each other. It was disturbing too being able to see dozens of armed security guards silhouetted around the auditorium – I think there were several important politicians in the audience. But none of that detracted from the magic of performing *Swan Lake* under a sky full of stars and with the sea, like Odette's lake, glinting in the background.

Critics may grumble at the company at home, but we nearly always sell out when we are abroad. Some of our audiences are very sophisticated and have obviously seen a lot of dance, so they know when to applaud particular technical points. Some give the impression that they don't know much about ballet at all but are determined to have a good time anyway, and then there are the polite ones which we dread. These audiences either aren't feeling any excitement at all, or else simply aren't expressing it in ways we understand. However the scariest audience I have ever danced in front of is the one which attended our opening of *Sleeping Beauty* in Washington in 1994.

This was the first night of a brand-new production of the ballet which meant that the company were nervous about having to try it out away from home. We'd had a particularly nightmarish dress rehearsal during which none of the scene changes had worked, and it didn't relax the atmosphere that we were also being filmed for the BBC documentary The House. Yet none of this compared with the terror of knowing that our first night gala was being attended by Bill Clinton and a crowd of important people from the White House. For we were not only going to be dancing in front of the world's most powerful man, but also in front of the world's press.

Looking back, the occasion seems almost farcical, since Clinton's presence meant that the security precautions had to be manic. A few hours before the show we had sniffer dogs everywhere, checking on and off stage for bombs, then during our warm-up there were security guards crawling all round the wings. Every time I came on or off stage I had to show a pass and at one point I thought I'd be dancing Aurora with one pinned to my tutu. At the same time the BBC's cameras were shadowing us even though I was yelling at them to please keep out of my sight. The tension wound up to such a pitch that by the time I was preparing for my first entrance I had become rigid with stage fright. I hadn't felt so nervous since I first became a professional dancer.

I was actually perched high up on a platform at this point (Aurora makes her entrance in this production down a steep flight of stairs) and all I wanted to do was disappear. My mind was playing terrifying tricks with me and letting me think, 'If I just let myself fall backwards now, then I won't have to go on and dance.'

But somehow I got myself down the stairs and on to the stage, and somehow the scenery managed not to stick and when the show ended we received a wonderful response from the audience. The company were on a high of relief and excitement and it's always the case when we're abroad, however strange or daunting our audiences, that we do get inspired by the fact that we are being seen and appreciated by so many new people.

At home in Covent Garden the ballet definitely suffers from being in the shadow of the opera company. Some of the reasons are political, some are cultural (dance is valued less in this country than in many places) but The Royal Opera also wields much more commercial power than we do. They can promote themselves through CD releases and through video (ballet unfortunately doesn't film as well as opera does) and stars like the Three Tenors have given opera such a huge international profile. I often feel that The Royal Ballet are too cautious about selling themselves and should be promoting their dancers more energetically as stars. When we go abroad we make a huge profit for the Opera House, in fact our tours are far more commercially competitive than the opera company's, and we have built up a worldwide reputation for ourselves. It's good for us to feel that we take priority for a change. It makes the dancers feel much more proud and assertive than we do in London.

When I go on my own to dance abroad, I also get a huge boost to my confidence. If I'm ever feeling a bit negative, a bit taken-for-granted in London, then the appreciation of a new audience can charge me up again. Since I've become well known as a principal I now receive many invitations to appear in galas and to make guest appearances with other companies. I accept them whenever my schedule allows, not only because of the extra money and the travel but because performing in different environments is such a revelation.

All companies develop their own working habits and all companies have their own particular faults and virtues, so going out of The Royal and into other companies, even for a few days, opens my eyes. I pick up a lot of technical information in class and rehearsal, spotting elements that I might want to incorporate into my own dancing, and I am also intrigued by the different ways in which other companies treat each other.

In Paris, for example, there is much fiercer competition between the dancers than at The Royal which makes for a less comfortable working environment than ours but produces dancers who are much hungrier for perfection. In New York City Ballet I notice that the dancers are much more up-front and like most New Yorkers they rarely apologize for themselves. If they have a big ego or a big mouth then that is just the way they are, and that confidence drives their dancing. At the same time they are also very direct about complimenting each other if they notice something that is good.

Unfortunately I've also come to learn how many talented dancers there are in the world today. When we stay at home we tend to get wrapped up in our own company, we accept our position within it and get comfortable with it, but when we go on trips abroad it's startling to realize that other companies have such varied standards, not always higher, but different. So the disadvantage of guesting is that I no longer actually enjoy my own dancing so much. The more brilliant dancers I see, the more dissatisfied I become with myself.

Performing in galas is generally my least favourite way of dancing abroad because the atmosphere backstage is always so competitive. There are usually a lot of big name dancers appearing in a single show together and everyone is ruthlessly jockeying for status. One major point of tension is finding out who will be dancing the flashiest pieces and will thus be likely to get the most applause. (The *Don Quixote* and *Corsaire pas de deux* are usually the most reliable show stoppers, even if they don't happen to be performed by the best dancers.) The other big issue is what order we will be dancing in. Everyone wants to perform last because the last dancers always get the most applause and remain most vividly in the audience's memory, and no one wants to go first because of course the audience haven't been warmed up. Some dancers I know will refuse point-blank to appear in a gala unless they get the final spot, and even though I don't care too desperately about being last I do hate having to perform first. My most depressing gala experience ever was opening a programme with the balcony scene from *Romeo and Juliet*. The *pas de deux* starts off very slowly, so the audience didn't settle down for ages, and it ends on a quiet note too, so we didn't even get much applause after we'd finished.

But I do prefer dancing serious duets rather than the more obvious gala show stoppers; I feel it is classier to perform a piece which has its own integrity and is not trying to milk the audience's applause. So I often choose to dance Balanchine's *Tchaikovsky Pas de Deux*, or the bedroom *pas de deux* from MacMillan's *Manon*, and Johnny and I have even done Chris Wheeldon's *Pavane* a few times.

Despite all the backstage machinations, galas *are* straightforward to dance in that all they involve is flying in for a couple of days with a partner and performing a familiar *pas de deux*. I find it's a very different experience making guest appearances with a company. Firstly, even though I'm usually dancing a role from one of the classics, I have to go into the company a few days early to learn their version of the ballet. (Even in *Swan Lake* or *Sleeping Beauty* details of the mime will always be different and some sections of the choreography may not even be the same.) Secondly, even though I'm usually dancing with a familiar partner, I also have to rehearse with the rest of the cast. This means that I'm thrown in at the deep end with unknown dancers and coaches, and when I danced with the Kirov in St Petersburg at the beginning of 1998 I did find myself viewed as a complete, and unwanted outsider.

I was dancing two performances of *La Bayadère* with Igor, who'd originally suggested the idea to the Kirov management. He was eager to show me off as his new partner (we guest a lot together) and I was naturally thrilled to be dancing with the company. No one from The Royal had performed with the Kirov since 1961, and it is one of the oldest and still one of the greatest companies in the world. The thought of appearing on the stage where Nijinsky, Pavlova and Nureyev had all danced was overwhelming.

When I left London I was naturally nervous, but I was buoyed up by the confidence of knowing I could dance the role of Nikiya well, and I was always very happy being partnered by Igor. However, I had quite a lot to learn about the Kirov's production of *Bayadère* and unfortunately some of the coaching set up for me didn't take place. Even when I *was* coached, the fact that I couldn't understand a word of Russian slowed rehearsals down and I was very unnerved because the coach had a way of speaking which made everything sound like an uncomplimentary remark – even when Igor assured me it wasn't.

Many of the dancers also made it plain that I wasn't welcome. The Kirov is a huge company, and most of its two hundred dancers have been trained at the great Vaganova school so the standard is very high. Obviously there is intense competition for roles and, as the dancers aren't accustomed to having many foreign guests, I think some of the principals thought I had a cheek coming in and taking two plum shows away from them. Few of them spoke to me or even smiled and at every rehearsal there was a group of them staring and whispering at everything I did. At least that's how it seemed to me, because the more alien I felt the more paranoid I became.

To make things worse, the Kirov stage has a very steep rake (or slope) which I had difficulty adjusting to in so short a time. There was one high lift in the ballet during which I thought I was about to fly out of my partner's hands and into the orchestra pit.

As my first show approached I became depressed and unable to sleep and on the night itself I was shaking with nerves. I wondered why I was doing this to myself, since the Kirov didn't seem to want me to be there. All I could do was focus on the fact that I was dancing on this magically historic stage, and get on with it.

Of course dancers in any company take a tough line with guests and expect them to prove themselves. At the Paris Opéra they're extremely hard to impress and show you exactly what they think of you. At New York City Ballet they also take a lot of convincing, in fact the first time I appeared with them in 1994 I knew they'd assumed in advance that I wouldn't be strong enough to perform with them. American dancers believe that the English are too soft and lyrical to dance Balanchine. But they were amazingly complimentary when they found that I could, in fact I've rarely known dancers be so appreciative. They kept saying that they really loved the way I used my arms because it was so different from theirs, and they were even asking me to leave The Royal and stay. They were saying, 'You're meant to dance with this company, we won't let you go.' I was astounded.

But when I guested with The Australian Ballet for a few days it was simply the best fun. The dancers genuinely wanted me to be there from the start and I didn't have to pass any kinds of tests. In fact I went to Melbourne directly after St Petersburg and the contrast couldn't have been greater. I walked around with a permanent grin on my face just thinking how nice it was to be liked.

6

PARTIES, POLO AND THE PAPARAZZI – CELEBRITY LIFE

I HAD MY first taste of press attention on the day I was told I would be leaving Sadler's Wells to become a soloist at The Royal. It was towards the end of the season, in 1988, and I was taken outside the theatre, still wearing my tracksuit, and a crowd of newspaper photographers began snapping photos of me. The pictures show me posing very obediently for the camera and smiling straight into the lens. But there's a dazed look at the back of my eyes. The events of the day had been so extraordinary that my thoughts and feelings were still in a whirl. I had no idea, then, what real media attention could be like and how it would begin to hone in on my career.

When I joined The Royal Ballet in September the limits

of my media ambitions were still, simply, to be on a company poster one day. I remember looking at a poster of Maria Almeida advertising one of our productions and thinking how beautiful she looked and how glamorous it would be to be on public view like that. But I couldn't imagine that it would happen to me.

Sixteen months later, when *Pagodas* was due to be premièred, I was a little less naïve but only a little. I began to attract a lot of press interest again and I was asked to do several photo shoots and some interviews. But they were all connected with the ballet and I still wasn't unsettled by the attention. It seemed part of the job of publicizing the company rather than reflecting any interest in me as a person. It was only later, after the ballet had opened, that I understood I was turning, or being turned, into a celebrity.

The first sign was the invitations. I started to receive invitations to galleries, fashion shows and shop openings and at first I kept trying to figure out why I had been invited. If I received an invitation to a new collection of glassware I'd be thinking, 'Oh perhaps they've created a glass statue of a ballet dancer or something.' Then I realized that the invitations didn't relate to my work at all, only to the number of times that a PR firm had seen my name or my picture in the press.

I don't know how many times they have to spot someone in the media before they decide to put him or her on one of their lists, but once you're on one PR list you start to appear on many others too. You get invitations to anything and everything so now, during the summer months in particular,

I'm often invited to about four functions a week. I'd have to retire from dancing to attend them all.

At the beginning of my career I was so thrilled to be asked that I used to go to nearly everything and it was fun. I frequently went by myself after work and since hardly anyone knew who I was then, these outings felt like private adventures. I loved being able to walk into a designer shop, look through all the new collections and stare at the other people there. There were often several well-known celebrities who turned up to these events, which were sometimes incredibly glamorous.

Of course I'd dress up myself, but having come straight from work I couldn't create the kind of extraordinary image some of the other women presented. At first I was totally wide-eyed, wondering how they had time to look so stylish. Then I realized that they'd mostly come from the hairdresser's and they had probably spent all day getting ready. This was what these women did, this was their job and there was usually a crowd of photographers ready to capture the results.

So I had my own secret glimpse into a different world, but after a while I began taking other people with me, to share in the gossip and the celebrity-spotting. In 1995 I was invited to the Dunhill polo match, and I took Angus and two other friends. It was such a spectacular event I needed some other people there to make it feel real. I was seated next to the singer Harry Connick Jnr. which I thought was extremely cool and Angus was sitting next to his wife. And while the polo itself didn't mean that much to me, I was very impressed by how beautiful and skilled the horses were. Most of all though I was entranced by the fabulous hats and by the whole social scene. I'd never experienced anything like it. There were nannies that had been specially hired to look after all the children, the Queen visited our tea-tent, and every guest was treated as if they were somebody grand, with a lavish lunch and tea and then a gift when we left.

I liked the fact that I could go to events like that and play at being someone different. I could dress up and mingle with famous people and it was all rather like going on to the stage. But I've come to learn that the social circuit can also be very competitive. In 1996 I went with a friend to the opening of the Fashion Cafe (owned by Naomi Campbell, Elle MacPherson and Claudia Schiffer), and it was almost vicious. We were made to feel uncomfortable from the start because we could only get into the party by walking along an elevated catwalk, with all the paparazzi crowded down the edges, flashing away at everyone. But once inside it felt even more unpleasant as we discovered there was one élite room reserved for all the promoters and supermodels and another room for everyone else. This created a horrible atmosphere in which a lot of desperate people were fighting to get into the smart room but being turned away by the bodyguards. At one point I was chatting to a major Australian pop star (I can't remember his name) until his minders suddenly clocked that he wasn't in the top celebrities' room and whisked him away.

So my friend and I decided to abandon that party and go to one which was being thrown the same evening by Donna Karan, to celebrate the opening of her new London shop. This one was held in a huge warehouse in Hammersmith, which had been decorated in extravagant style. It was all in black, except for a white dance floor up one end and some ice bars at the other end serving fish and noodles. There were three black pillars in the middle of the room and a mass of candles which glowed wonderfully behind black gauze. All around the edges were black sofas, and since the party was full of models it naturally turned out to be a constant catwalk. Everyone spent half the time sitting on the sofas watching other people walk around then they'd get up and walk around in front of everyone else.

At these kinds of events I can blend in with the crowd and gossip with my friends – there's a constant buzz of, 'Have you seen so and so? Look, she's wearing Gucci shoes, how did she get them, there's a waiting list for those' – but at more formal events like dinners I'm at the mercy of the seating arrangement and if the guests sitting next to me don't recognize me then they may not even bother to talk. I feel embarrassed about advertising who I am to people who don't know, so often when I introduce myself I'll just say that I work for The Royal Ballet. This obviously doesn't impress them, so sometimes my neighbour simply turns round and speaks to the person on their other side all evening.

But the social mix at these events is often fascinating. In 1996 I was invited to a dinner at Quaglino's restaurant to celebrate an anniversary of Tiffany's (though I'd never bought anything from their shop) and I arrived right behind Jerry Hall and Marie Helvin. They made a big entrance together. Marie Helvin was wearing an extraordinary Versace dress – transparent except for the pockets over the breasts – and Jerry's hair was enormous. The paparazzi went so wild for them I began to question what I was doing there. I'm not a supermodel, I'm not a film star and I'm not a socialite who lives her life on the party circuit. But at least Angus was with me and when we made our own entrance down that lovely grand staircase in Quaglino's I saw two photographers I knew. It's always a relief to see a couple of friendly faces and these men have always been very nice to me, they always shout, 'Hi, Darcey, how are you?' and they're not aggressive like some of the paparazzi.

I've never become completely used to having my photo taken in public and sometimes, when there's a large crowd of photographers surrounding me, it's very intimidating. All I can see are flashes popping off and voices shouting, 'Here, here, Darcey, look at me, here.' I hate it, and I often hate seeing the pictures themselves when they're displayed in the party sections of glossy magazines. When I first appeared in the glossies I have to admit I was very overexcited to see myself there, but as the years have gone by I don't seem to have got any better at posing for them. I always appear to be pulling faces, because I seem to get photographed when I'm in the middle of talking to someone. Some people seem to know exactly where the cameras are all the time and even when they're chatting they maintain perfectly composed expressions. I haven't got the knack.

For the Tiffany's dinner I'd arrived, as usual, having managed only a quick shower after work. But I was wearing a lovely frock which had been lent to me by the designer Neil Cunningham, so at least I looked the part. It was very

Audrey Hepburn, in chocolate brown satin with a knee-length skirt and a V neck that was ruched up and held in a *diamanté* clasp. I was wearing long brown gloves to match and brown chiffon round my shoulders so I felt extremely glamorous.

Angus and I were seated at a table with the son of an American business tycoon, a Greek shipping magnate and a socialite model who, fortunately, turned out to be a very chatty group of people. Unfortunately though, I couldn't stop myself being distracted by the model who must have been over six foot tall and was wearing a dress slit right up to her hip bone. She kept standing up to wave at people and I couldn't work out how she stayed decent because she didn't seem to be wearing any underwear.

The social world has some strange rituals. There were many seriously rich people at this dinner but I noticed that everyone became very excited when we were given our complimentary gifts at the end of the evening, comparing what they'd each been given. I also suspected a few were sneaking some of the Tiffany glass ashtrays which had been left on all the tables into their handbags.

These days I don't have the stamina for so much partying as I need to have evenings to myself at home with Angus or with friends. Of course I love the glamour of these big events, they remind me of old black-and-white movies with everyone so elaborately dressed up, and I find them visually very appealing. But the image has become tarnished for me as I've realized how much snobbery and competition revolve around the social circuit.

In any case I can also get my glamour fix from doing fashion shoots for magazines, which are a wonderful way of indulging my love of dressing up (my old dressing-up box has a lot to answer for). I adore the fact that I can sit down for an hour while a hairstylist and make-up artist create a series of amazingly different looks for me. In the fashion world this is considered work. But compared with what we do at The Royal it seems a luxurious way of earning money.

Shoots can be physically demanding though because when photographers and editors decide to use dancers, rather than models, it's usually because they want us to do extreme things with our bodies.

For example, one of my first shoots (for *Vogue*) involved a week in New York where I was being photographed with the American ballerina Cynthia Harvey. The strain on us both was quite intense. We had to get up early to do class every morning as the photographer essentially wanted us to dance for the camera. Then we'd spend the whole of the rest of the day working out poses, having our hair and make-up changed and putting on different clothes. The shoot lasted for six days.

Fashion photographers are often amazed by dancers' stamina but of course, as a breed, we've been brought up to please. It's been drilled into us to obey our teacher, our coach and our director so we naturally tend to do anything we're asked by photographers too. We'll work very long hours for them and we're not precious about how we look.

In New York they'd virtually called a halt to shooting on the final day when I pointed out that there was one more outfit left and suggested a few more ideas that we could try out. This is not normal model behaviour. But I was very excited by the whole business and those last photographs actually turned out to be the best. By that point I knew we'd nearly finished and I could risk experimenting with some wild jumps for the camera. I remember thinking, 'I really love doing this. I could do this all the time.'

Since then I've taught myself even more about the modelling business and I still enjoy doing shoots. But I never let them get in the way of my dancing, so I'll only schedule them for the holidays, weekends or a free day. Right from the beginning of my career I laid down the rule that I would never miss an important class or rehearsal. The only reason I get this kind of extra work is because I'm well-known in my profession, so it would be self-defeating to let my work suffer.

Sometimes, if I'm being put into really outrageous clothes for a shoot, I also wonder if I should be being more careful of my image. Are PVC trousers and heavy black make-up a good advert for a ballerina? But the way dancers dress today is a much more accurate reflection of the people we are, we don't have to pretend to be perfect princesses the way previous generations did. I know that sometimes I disappoint members of the public because I don't look like Margot Fonteyn. She always appeared beautiful and untouchable wherever she went, but her style isn't mine.

Even so, one of the most interesting series of fashion shoots I've ever done made me feel a lot like Margot. They had been arranged to publicize an exhibition of wartime and

New Look fashion being held at the Imperial War Museum in 1997, and I had been asked to model some of the original Dior creations.

The first shoot was for the exhibition poster and catalogue cover and for that I'd been given permission to wear Dior's famous Bar Suit. It had been sent all the way from Paris and when I first tried it on it was like handling a work of art. When it arrived at my dressing room at the Opera House (so that I could try it on between rehearsals) it was packed with so much protective material that the boxes were too big to fit inside the room. We all had to wear little gloves to handle the suit in order to keep the oils from our skin off the material and when I put it on it felt amazing. The jacket was slightly boned and had padding at the hips to create the New Look. It was also nipped in severely at the waist but it was so beautifully made that it felt really comfortable. When I put on the straw hat and the little gloves as well, I felt like a million dollars.

For the actual photo shoot I had my hair and make-up done in pure '40s style and the photographer, Lord Snowdon, had a very stylized set built out of white columns, with some wisps of smoke to give a post-war feel. I had to balance between the columns on a tiny shelf, and hold my pose for hours until he got the shot he wanted. Snowdon is a total perfectionist (a fact I knew from long experience as he took some of my first professional ballet photos) and the next day I ached all over.

The organizers of the exhibition had been lent a lot of other Dior clothes too because the event was tied in with

Dior's fiftieth anniversary. One of these was Margot Fonteyn's wedding coat which was beautiful, but which unfortunately I wasn't permitted to wear. But some of the others I modelled for a shoot with the *Evening Standard* magazine. The make-up artist was a genius and gave me a total Audrey Hepburn look while the clothes themselves made me feel like a movie star. For pure style, the late 1940s and early 1950s are my favourite era.

For some of the other shoots though, I was posing in the wartime fashions and although these were less glamorous than the Diors they were still extraordinary. Some outfits had been made by ordinary people, during the war, and they'd managed to create fabulously original pieces of clothing out of nothing. There was an evening dress made out of parachute material, a Japanese silk map that had been transformed into a shirt, and an old dressing-gown, which actually looked more like a ball dress, made out of material that was printed all over with little maps of England. I discovered that each one had a story to tell, and it was so touching to think of all these women desperately trying to look stylish during such a grim time. One outfit was a beautiful nightdress which a woman had sewn to wear when her husband returned from the war. She'd been told the exact day and time he was meant to arrive so she'd got herself all dressed up in the nightdress ready for him. But she'd waited and waited and he hadn't turned up. Then the next day he'd walked through the door while she was scrubbing the floor in her old work clothes.

There's no question that modelling is a lot of fun and I

feel lucky to get so many opportunities, but I do also feel very intimidated when I find myself having to work with professional models. Two years ago I was offered a contract with Mulberry to launch their new perfume and I was given some amazing perks as part of the deal. I had to be seen in public wearing Mulberry clothes and accessories – which I was given free – and I had some rooms in my new house decorated for a Mulberry interiors photo. But I was also asked to do a couple of fashion shows which involved walking down the same catwalk as models like Yasmine Le Bon and these made me feel a hopeless amateur. I'm very confident in my own work, because I know exactly what my strengths and weaknesses are, but when I step into someone else's profession I'm ready to fall apart. I'm terrified of making myself look ridiculous when I'm put alongside experts.

I feel especially nervous when I'm asked to make speeches and give out awards as I tend to freeze if I have to say something formal in front of an audience. I recently had to present an award for Live Comics and on this occasion, although I'd got my little speech ready, I'd forgotten I was being filmed for television. As I spoke I was smiling out at the audience the whole time, instead of staring into Camera One, or whoever was filming me. Mistakes like these make me feel badly out of my depth. But if I never pushed myself into new situations I'd never find out what I'm capable of. I hate to be a coward – even though I give myself some embarrassing moments.

One of the strangest spinoffs from my celebrity status has, without doubt, been the experience of modelling for my own waxwork in 1997. When the people at Madame Tussauds asked if I would like to be done, I naturally felt very flattered. I was going to be placed in among some extremely famous men and women. But I also found the idea of being made into a dummy very disconcerting and, as I discovered, the process of being modelled was most peculiar.

Anthony Dowell had persuaded me to pose as Aurora, from *Sleeping Beauty*, in one of the attitude balances from the Rose Adage, and when I went for the first sitting I found that I had to hold the position for *two hours*. There was a pole, nailed to the floor, which went up the length of my supporting leg, and another pole which held up my back leg, so at least I wasn't going to fall over. But there were about six people moving round to measure me as I stood there, and the process took much longer than usual because they weren't sure what to do about my leg muscles. The fact that I was leaning against a pole rather than supporting my own weight meant that the muscles had gone soft, and were a completely different shape from how they would be in a true balance.

During the sitting there were also several photographers taking photos of me from every angle, and for them I had to balance on my own, without the poles, so that I looked exactly as I would on stage. Even though they were very solicitous about letting me stop and relax when I needed to, I was still unable to move the next day. My back had completely seized up from holding the same position for so long.

At a later sitting, moulds were taken of my feet and hands, which felt even stranger. I had to put on my point shoe and then place my foot in a bucket while a lukewarm rubbery solution was poured around my foot to make the mould. This took about five minutes to set, after which they cut down one side and I had to wiggle my foot and slowly draw it out. While it was setting the rubber felt horrible and I felt anxious because I'd lost all sense of what position my foot was in. It would look terrible if my waxwork dummy was balancing on a sickled foot.

Then we went through the same process with my hands, and it was even harder to keep my fingers in the right position with the pressure from the rubber solution. The people at Tussauds promised to send the hands over when they were finished so that I could check them, which was reassuring as they had already had problems with one of my legs. On the model, my kneecap had come out too long and my shin too short, so that it looked as if my knee had fallen down my leg. They explained how hard I was for them to model because they weren't used to dancers – the last one to be done had been Nureyev, who was years ago. Usually their models have clothes on so they don't have to worry about the correct look of their back muscles or the way that the knee is pulled up when they're standing on one leg.

When my model was unveiled, I was allowed in to see it about five minutes ahead of all the photographers so I could get over the shock of it alone. And the shock was tremendous. My mother was with me and, in order to reach the room where my dummy was we had to walk down a very

Amores
© *Leslie E Spatt*

With Jonathan Cope in *Romeo and Juliet*, my favourite ballet
© *Leslie E Spatt*

Rehearsing with Zoltan Solymosi
© *Anthony Crickmay*

From *The Farewell Pas De Deux* in *Winter Dreams*
© Leslie E Spatt

Taking a moment's respite from the Ugly Sisters!
© Bill Cooper

Guesting at the New York City Ballet,
danceing with Jock Soto in George Balanchine's *Agon*

Photography © Paul Kolnik. Choreography by George Balanchine
© The George Balanchine Trust

Dancing *La Bayadère* with Igor Zelensky
© Bill Cooper

My Dior experience with Lord Snowdon

© *Snowdon*

Me as 'The Hostess'
© *David Sheinmann*

My favourite publicity shot for Mulberry
© Tim Richmond

imposing corridor lined with models of international heads of state. At the end we came face to face with the British royal family grouped in front of red velvet curtains (though I noticed Diana and Fergie had been placed discreetly to one side). Then we turned the corner and I froze – because there I was, balancing high on a pedestal, looking down at me.

Every other model in the room was at floor level so I was dominating the whole room (despite the fact that it contained celebrities as impressive as George Solti and Torvill and Dean); I wished I had been tucked more discreetly into a corner, and I also wished that I didn't look quite so real. When I looked closely at my model it was just like looking in the mirror. Tussauds had cast even my teeth and ears, so every detail of my appearance was frighteningly accurate. The experience was so surreal that I wanted to get out of the room as quickly as possible. It felt to me that this was the dummy's world, not mine, and that I was the imposter.

When I looked around the rest of the exhibition I realized that I did in fact look a lot more realistic than some of the other models (apparently some have to be made from photographs as the subjects can't or won't give up their time to sit). My feeling that I was less real than the wax Darcey increased at the unveiling party where the other guests kept wanting to pose for photographs with my dummy rather than with me. I've since discovered that what fascinates the public most is looking up the skirt of my tutu. People are intrigued by dancers' tutus as they are such complicated garments, but of course audiences don't normally have the chance to look up a ballerina's skirt. I often get younger dancers in the company coming up to me and asking if I can sign a photo of someone they know with my model. Invariably, their friend is looking up my tutu.

The spookiest feature of this whole affair was discovering that my model may survive for only five years – depending on how my career goes – and that when it comes to be scrapped it will be melted down! I was shocked – it felt as though they were planning to kill me off. I asked at Tussauds if I could take my dummy home with me when they no longer wanted it and they seemed very surprised, as apparently no one usually asks. They couldn't figure out where I would put it, so I asked if I could at least just keep my head!

Tussauds turned out to be a long episode in my diary (it took about ten sittings), and it threw up a lot of surprises. When I take on outside commitments which only involve dancing I expect life to be more normal. But when I performed at the Royal Variety Show in 1997 I felt as if fate wasn't on my side.

I'd been asked to dance the balcony *pas de deux* from *Romeo and Juliet* with Johnny Cope, and the event began to look jinxed from the moment Johnny got himself injured in his motorbike accident. I had to find myself another partner fast, and luckily Stuart Cassidy agreed to help me out. This was sweet of him as he wasn't entirely confident that he was tall enough to partner me in this *pas de deux*. But as dancers we knew how to adapt ourselves and it was only when we arrived at the Dominion Theatre for our first rehearsal that our real headaches began.

The first was the scenery they'd produced for us, which was a bizarre-looking balcony and a backdrop depicting Tuscan countryside in the daytime. We tried to explain that the balcony scene takes place at night, in Verona, but it was too late for them to get it right.

The second was the floor, which had been painted with white emulsion and was extremely slippery to dance on. Of course we knew that the Variety Show was geared up for musicians and rock bands rather than for ballet dancers, but even so we'd obviously injure ourselves badly if we slipped. We sprinkled the floor with rosin and had to accept the crew's promise that they would try to repaint the floor and produce a grittier surface by the time we came to perform. But when we started rehearsing we realized we'd never be able to dance the choreography full out anyway as the stage was much smaller than we'd expected and it also had a slight rake. Finally, we were getting very apprehensive about our conductor, Paul Stobard. Though he was a wonderful pianist he hadn't had much experience as a conductor, particularly with a commercial orchestra, and he rehearsed our music much too fast. He admitted that he was very nervous and kept cracking jokes about how the orchestra had never played any classical music before. 'They'll be useless doing Prokofiev,' he said. We didn't laugh.

On the day of the performance, Cassidy and I had rehearsals at Baron's Court so we couldn't get to the Dominion Theatre until after three o'clock in the afternoon. As soon as we arrived we were whisked on stage to dance our *pas de deux* for the cameras, as the show was being televised live that night. Since there wasn't time to change we did the whole balcony scene in our jeans, and we then had to run through the finale with all the other celebrities.

This only left us time for a very quick rehearsal in costume and we were beginning to feel extremely uncertain about the show. We still didn't know each other well in this *pas de deux* and the floor didn't seem any less slippery. There's a moment where Juliet has to run downstairs from the balcony, go out into the wings and come flying back on again for Romeo to catch her. Each time I tried to do this I slipped just before I got on stage which ruined the timing, and the drama of my entrance. We had to hope that we could spread enough rosin on the floor just before our slot.

It turned out that we weren't dancing until the second half of the show so I had time to jump into a cab and race over to Neil Cunningham's in Piccadilly to pick up a dress. I needed one to wear for the finale and for the dinner that was being held at the Dorchester afterwards. Neil knew exactly which frock I needed to hold my own in a stageful of stars and lent me a long navy-blue version of the dress I wore to the Tiffany's dinner at Quaglino's. Fortunately it didn't need any alterations, so I could zoom straight back to the theatre and get ready early.

I wanted to see as much of the show as possible, for even though I was fretting about my own performance I loved the idea of appearing in a programme full of showbiz names. Bob Monkhouse was presenting, Tom Jones was doing the finale, Joan Rivers, Jim Davidson, Joaquin Cortez were all performing numbers and Lionel Richie was making a surprise appearance. There were also extracts from various musicals, and even the Moscow State Circus – I was amazed that they could organize so many people together in one show.

Unfortunately, the theatre wasn't big enough to hold all the performers backstage so the poor chorus dancers had to change outside in portacabins and then make their way back into the theatre. This was complicated because Prince Charles was attending the show and security was very tight. I was one of the lucky performers with a dressing room, which I turned out to be sharing with Pauline and Linda from Birds of a Feather. They were fabulous company backstage, very sweet and funny, and they kept assuring me that they were terrified even though they'd been performing since they were five years old.

When the show started, Cassidy and I watched from the wings. It was very entertaining but we began to wonder why we'd been asked to perform our romantic *pas de deux*. We were far more classical in style than all the other dance numbers and our costumes would look so odd next to all the chorus girls in their little blonde wigs. When we finally went on stage I sensed straightaway that the audience did find us a strange contrast and I wished that we'd chosen to dance a jazzier number. Still, they were very appreciative.

In fact they were having such a good time and clapped so enthusiastically throughout that several of the performers indulged themselves. Tom Jones was only meant to sing for ten minutes but he carried on for at least twenty, and as a result the show ran for an extra hour and didn't end until eleven thirty. Poor Angus had been waiting in the car to come with me to the Dorchester dinner, but by the time we left the theatre it was far too late. I had to get up for work the next day, and couldn't afford to party all night, even though I badly wanted to introduce Pauline and Linda to Angus. As a dancer I'm used to being self-disciplined. It's become automatic for me that work takes priority during the week even though it means missing out on some of the glitzier aspects of my job.

In addition to live performances I take on quite a lot of television and video work, though dancing for the camera is, I've discovered, far more gruelling than dancing on stage. It is time-consuming because it requires the dancers to repeat the steps constantly, stopping and starting for the cameras, the lights or the music. It is physically taxing too because our muscles get rock hard when we work so erratically and it becomes difficult to move properly. It's also difficult to feel that we are giving a real performance, yet it's always important to me that I dance my best on film because I'm reaching so much wider an audience through television than I do on stage. Few people can afford to go to the Opera House regularly and the majority of the public know so little about ballet. They think that it's all tutus and *Swan Lake*s and aren't aware that we have a large repertoire of modern work as well.

A typical filming day (complete with its typical headaches) was one that I did with Igor for Carlton television, when we danced Balanchine's *Tchaikovsky Pas de*

Deux. I had to take my ten thirty morning class in London but was then driven up to Carlton's studios in Nottingham with my coach, Donald MacLeary. (I'd paid Donald to come and watch the filming as I needed his vigilant eye to ensure I wasn't looking bad for the camera. It's not unusual to work your heart out for a piece of filming, and then die when you finally see yourself on screen because you've been made to look so odd.)

I met Igor up in Nottingham and we started rehearsing at five o'clock, which compared with my usual routine felt a very late hour to start. We had three hours of filming ahead of us and while I was getting changed I watched Igor doing a run-through of his solo on a TV monitor and I could see there were going to be problems. He kept disappearing off the screen because his jump is so high and the cameras couldn't move far enough back in the studio to keep him in frame.

I was worrying about myself too because I only had one pair of shoes I was comfortable with and I was nervous that they might go soft on me if we had to run through the ballet too many times. I'd meant to sew another pair on the drive up but had been so tired I'd fallen asleep instead. Also, when I saw the backdrop of the studio my jaw dropped as it had been painted a pale lilac with a moon and clouds. I didn't know what the Balanchine Trust would think of it as they are terribly fussy about how Balanchine's works are performed. When we dance this *pas de deux* at the Opera House we have a dark blue backdrop – very plain and classical.

But there was no time to change anything before the filming. We had decided to break the ballet into several sections as we filmed. We'd mark each one for spacing and height of lifts, then perform it for the cameras before going on to the next section. Luckily I only had to run my solo once before they filmed it, but Igor again had problems fitting his jumps on to screen and by the time we came to dance the coda we were exhausted. It was ten o'clock at night and we hadn't taken a single break. I still had my *fouettés* to film and by then I was finding it difficult to turn, especially as I'd started to get a runny nose. This does not produce a dignified effect when you are whipping your head round at speed. I kept having to stop and blow it, then they had to powder my nose because it had become so red and raw. We finally stopped at ten thirty to film curtain calls and I discovered that all this time a poor little boy (who can only have been about six years old) had been kept waiting to give me the flowers.

It was much more fun being in front of the cameras for the French and Saunders show. This came about after Jennifer and Dawn had decided they wanted to write a ballet skit for their series and had asked Anthony if they could watch us rehearse and pick up some local colour. Luckily for them, Patricia Neary from New York City Ballet happened to be coaching us in *Apollo* when they arrived and she's as colourful a ballet character as you can get! Even though she now has two false hips, she still demonstrates every step, and along with her spectacles she wears very traditional New York City Ballet practice clothes, pretty pink leg warmers and a chiffon skirt, which she changes several times during a rehearsal. Dawn and Jennifer lapped it up, they thought that this was exactly the way a ballet mistress should be.

After rehearsal, they asked me if I wanted to be in their sketch and I was delighted. They were very concerned to reassure me that they would be laughing *with* me rather than *at* me, but I didn't need any persuading. I was a huge fan of theirs and so, it turned out, was Anthony. While we were in his office discussing the show Anthony gently butted in and asked if he could be in it too. Dawn and Jennifer were obviously thrilled but even so, when Anthony and I made our entrance into the sketch their first line was, 'Oh, Miss Bussell, you didn't have to bring your father too.'

They were wickedly funny, and Anthony and I couldn't stop laughing all the way through the filming. We'd been given a script to look at but at every take they changed the lines slightly. The alterations kept Dawn and Jennifer fresh as actresses but they made Anthony and I even more hopeless at keeping our faces straight. We had to repeat one take over and over again because Anthony got into such uncontrollable hysterics. Our names kept deviating wildly so that I never knew whether I was going to be addressed as Miss Bristle or Busty or Busstop, while Anthony was Tone or Sir T. We loved it.

Last year I made another cameo appearance for Dawn on her Vicar of Dibley series, which arose out of a duet she and I had done together at a charity gala organized by Wayne Sleep. We'd choreographed it together with the help of Gail Taphouse, one of our ballet mistresses at The Royal, and it involved me performing a solo which she, as my reflection in a mirror, had to try and copy. Dawn is a very good dancer and she went for every step even though she made it all look so ridiculous. Towards the end of the dance she had to storm out of the mirror and insist that it was her turn, which left me trying to copy her very Dawn-like disco routine.

Dawn later decided that she wanted to include this duet in her TV series, so she wrote a scene in which I appear in my car, listening to the radio as her character is being interviewed about a village festival she's running. In the scene I'm meant to be driving to Broadcasting House myself, so when I get there I inevitably bump into Dawn and offer to help her out. This set up the later episode when I appear doing the mirror dance in the village hall. In the gala version of the duet Dawn turned very nasty on me right at the end, but she thought that as a vicar she'd have to be more pleasant otherwise the public would complain – so we changed the ending to something sweeter.

I actually have to go to the BBC regularly because The Royal's press department are always keen for me to squeeze in as many TV, radio and newspaper interviews as possible. These are good publicity for the company and I'm always happy to talk about my work, but I hate it when journalists push me to talk about my private life instead.

Once I was asked to appear on The Big Breakfast, which was an adventure in itself as the show was filmed somewhere on a North London estate and it took hours and hours to find. I'd completely lost track of where we were going, and when we finally arrived the studios turned out to be completely surreal. They were located in a perfectly normal-looking house except that it was stuck by itself in the middle of a wilderness of offices and warehouses. Once inside I was ushered into what looked like an ordinary living room and given a cup of tea, and I thought I'd been left there to wait until it was time to go on set. But then suddenly the whole crew rushed in, took my tea away and said, 'Right, Darcey, are you ready to go?' I felt like Alice at the Mad Hatter's Tea Party.

Vanessa Feltz was interviewing me and I'd told the producer at the beginning that I didn't want her to ask personal questions. But of course it was live TV and she went ahead and asked them anyway – starting off with questions about Angus, who I'd recently become engaged to. The funny thing was, as soon as she'd asked the questions she'd say, 'Oh, I suppose you don't want to talk about that, do you,' and then she'd answer them all herself, before I had a chance to open my mouth. During the whole interview she talked so fast that I could hardly get a word in. It was as if she was performing a set routine that didn't have anything to do with her guests.

Other journalists don't give up so easily though, particularly the ones from the tabloids, and however hard I insist that I'm not talking about my private life they keep slipping the subject back into conversation. To me this seems very unprofessional. The public only know about me because of my work on stage, not because of what happens in my private life, so I don't think it's relevant to talk to them about Angus or my family. In fact it's important to me that they remain separate from the theatre. Of course I'll chat about my day to Angus but I don't want him to become too involved in all its details as I want to forget about work in the evening – and so does he. He has a demanding job in the City and needs time to relax as much as I do. The time we can spend alone together is precious.

I also think that talking about my private life destroys the magic of what I do on stage. My job is to go up there and create an illusion of ease and grace – not to talk about how I've just had a row with my husband. I know that people are interested in the private lives of celebrities, but I prefer to protect my family and my friends. It simply isn't fair to expect them to deal with people coming up and saying to them, 'Ooh, I read this or that about you.'

Unfortunately, even if I won't speak about certain subjects to journalists I can't stop them from making things up. When journalists approach me at public events I've learnt to say just a few bland words and nothing more, but they still go on and invent quotes which are not only inaccurate, but stupid and trivial. I remember being very upset by something I read in one of the tabloid diaries where the journalist claimed to have chatted to me at some function. He said that I'd talked to him about how I felt I had plenty of time to have children in the future because right now I just wanted to have a good time with my husband. The tone was very insinuating and when I read items like that I get depressed as they make me sound so cheap. I try to harden myself and tell myself that even if it matters to me, the readers themselves will only glance at the article for a few seconds. The rest of the world have their own lives to think about, they don't care whether I want to have babies or not.

One of my worst experiences with the press was when I was withdrawn from dancing *Manon* and the story was blown up on the front page of some papers. It made me understand how media attention can go to people's heads and delude them into thinking that their lives are of national importance. For a split second I really believed I *was* big news. But since this took place at the time of the Gulf War it didn't take long for me to realize how ridiculous it all was. My story was just about a few ballet dancers and a performance, it wasn't a world event.

I also came to resent the press around the time of my wedding, in August 1997, when I was constantly being questioned about when and where it was going to be held. On one occasion I'd agreed to do a photo shoot to publicize a gala which was being staged to raise money for the re-building of the Opera House. I was posing with Placido Domingo in front of a model of the new building but instead of talking about the Opera House the reporters kept asking me about my wedding. I was mortified, it looked as if I was trying to publicize myself, but Placido was very charming about it and wished me luck for my marriage. One of the papers ran a photo of us, with the headline *So This is the Happy Couple – Not!*

Both *Hello!* and *OK!* wanted to run pieces about my wedding, but I was determined to keep it secret. I'd opted to have a quiet wedding in the country with just family and close friends around me, and I desperately didn't want any paparazzi finding out where it was and ruining my day. After the event I was willing to let a magazine use a couple of the photos to illustrate an interview with me, but otherwise my wedding day wasn't for sale.

I can also feel hounded by the pressure to look good for photographers whenever I'm attending public events. I sympathize with Princess Diana's need to look immaculate all the time, the press expected it of her and they'd have given her a bad time if she wasn't. But I don't see the press as an enemy. They are a fact of life, they go with the job, and if I'm going to be in the public eye I have to accept them.

I don't feel too bothered either when people stop me in the shops or out on the street. It feels a bit odd but usually they are pleasant and don't attempt to harass me in any way. The only time I really want to be invisible is when I come out of the theatre feeling especially tired or depressed that I've done a bad show. It is late at night and all I want to do is go home, have a bath and go to bed, and it's hard to deal with a crowd of people waiting at the stage door, all hoping to speak to me and to take pictures.

I feel guilty about not wanting to see them because I know that they are my real fans. These are the people who have followed my career and watched many of my shows, so of course it's a privilege to have them waiting for me. The least I can do is smile and be pleasant. But sometimes I do feel like slipping out of another door, especially if I know that I've got a hard week ahead of me.

I drive home by car after a show because it can be difficult to get taxis at that time of night, and I don't want to risk having to go on the tube when I still have half my stage make-up on and my flowers to carry. People would stare and think, 'Either she's mad or she's famous. And if she *is* famous, why is she travelling on the underground?' It would also be very disorienting getting into the train after I've just been dancing a role like Giselle or Aurora.

Finding time to fit in all the extra commitments that come with being a celebrity is impossible. I get asked to open charity events, speak at functions, hand out awards, sponsor good causes, do all kinds of photo shoots and publicity stunts – I've even been offered a couple of Honorary Doctorates. Of course I have to turn down a lot of these just to maintain a private life and sometimes, if I'm feeling tired or low, I do start envying other people's lives. After a hard day's work all that I'm fit for is soaking my feet in a hot bath and when I see people walking round the shops, or couples going out to have lunch together, I can feel as if I spend my whole life rushing between rehearsals and performances and press work. It doesn't seem right. Nicky Tranah, one of my close friends in the company, has a beautiful daughter who I'm godmother to. But I hardly ever have the chance to see her.

I also have several projects on the go at home, which I always wish I had more time for. When I was recovering from my foot surgery I taught myself how to work with mosaics and I've created a large mosaic for my living room fireplace and one for the bathroom wall. I find the medium so exciting that I've had to make myself slow down or the whole house would be covered. I'm very interested in interior design generally, and when we moved into our new house in 1997 I became very involved in planning the colours and furnishings and making architectural sketches for the alterations. I sometimes fantasize about training to be an architect when I've retired from ballet – except that it's a seven-year course. While I'm on holiday I also have time for my most passionate hobby, which is sketching and painting watercolours. I can pass several hours with my sketchpad drawing people or landscapes.

When I'm at home I rarely watch television, nor do I have music playing all the time. I enjoy music – from Lenny Kravitz to Mozart's *Requiem* – and I've recently gone back to practising my old instrument, the guitar. But as I work with music all day I like to have some silence at home.

On free evenings Angus and I go to the cinema quite often. I adored films like *Il Postino* and *The Hairdresser's Husband* but I do have a weakness for Hollywood trash. It's perfect, and necessary, escapism. We also eat out with friends a lot, and one reason why I enjoy the fact that Angus doesn't work in the theatre is that he introduces me to people who aren't dancers.

I've always kept up with a little group of friends from home and primary school, even while they've gone off to university and scattered off into different careers. But during the year that I was touring with Sadler's Wells I found it hard to make new friends outside dance because I spent so much time on the road. Even when I returned to London to work at The Royal, my working hours were still unsociable. I was actually introduced to Angus through a fellow dancer in The Royal, who invited him with several other friends to a show and asked me to have dinner with them afterwards.

It's very easy for dancers to get lodged into their own little world, yet even though this can make me feel claustrophobic I never want to leave it far behind. When I go away on holiday I start to get bored after a couple of weeks and can't wait to get back to the studio. I would also be crazy not to love the perks that come with my profession. A couple of years ago Audi offered me one of their brand-new cars to drive for six months in return for promoting it, and as I love cars that was a perfect treat. Another bonus are the designer clothes which I'm allowed to borrow for public functions and which give me licence for lots more dressing up

I have a close relationship with the designer Neil Cunningham, who got in touch with me a couple of years ago to ask if I wanted to wear some of his designs, and when he brought over his portfolio I was thrilled. His dresses are lovely, very classically elegant and I've worn several of them since (he also designed my wedding dress). He has a group of wonderfully skilled assistants working for him who can alter a dress to fit me in a single day, and this is a huge advantage as I'm very bad at planning ahead.

In theory I am meant to look at my diary in advance, list the functions which are coming up and then approach designers to see if they can lend me anything. But often I forget to do this until the week before and that's not enough notice if the clothes have to be sent from abroad or they have to be altered to fit. Obviously no designer is going to lend an outfit if it doesn't look as good as possible on me, otherwise it's not good publicity for them.

I still feel rather intimidated about approaching some of the big houses – the idea of ringing up Armani and casually asking them to loan me a frock seems a bit of a nerve – but I have, on occasion, been lent clothes by very grand houses like Yves Saint Laurent and Chanel, in fact Chanel offered to give me one of their suits to keep as a going away outfit for my wedding. Bruce Oldfield and Jasper Conran have also been very good about lending me clothes, and I wore a very gorgeous one of Bruce's, with a sequinned top and chiffon skirt, for the party after our opening performance of *Sleeping Beauty* in Washington.

Despite all the trauma of getting the show on to the stage, that night turned out to be a memorable one for the company because both the Clintons came on stage afterwards to meet us. I was impressed by Bill Clinton, who had a much more imposing presence than I'd registered on TV. He seemed very, very big, and good-looking and Hillary too looked very glamorous. They were both easy and charming and chatted to a lot of the cast about the show. I asked them what their daughter Chelsea had thought, since I knew she was very enthusiastic about ballet, but it was Bill Clinton's conversation with Fiona Chadwick, our Lilac Fairy, which was reported throughout the press the next day. He had joked to her that he 'could do with a Lilac Fairy' himself at the White House, 'to put everything right,' and Fiona had grinned and said, 'I'll come round any time, with my magic wand.'

The Clintons posed for photographs with us all and I still have a copy pinned to my wall. I'm standing on one side of Bill and on the other is Stephen Wicks as Carabosse, who is posing with his hand dangling evilly over the President's shoulder. Unfortunately the Clintons couldn't come to the party afterwards, but it was still a very big function, with a band, a proper dance floor and masses to eat and drink.

It is part of our job to go to functions like these as they are filled with sponsors who've supported our productions. But grateful as we are for their donations a party is sometimes the last thing dancers feel like after a long show. Having just stripped off all our make-up and costumes, we don't want to get dressed up again. However, when we're on tour no one can keep us away from the parties. We are paid a daily sum to cover our expenses and food, from which most of us try and save a little to take home or go shopping with. So even the company stars don't turn up their noses at a free meal.

My grandest social event, though, must be the day I attended Buckingham Palace to collect my OBE in 1995. Several months previously I'd been to a party at 10 Downing Street with a crowd of other sporting and theatre stars and I'd met John Major and chatted a little. But I had so little idea that I was in line for an OBE that when I first got the letter telling me so, I completely failed to understand it. I assumed that the fact I was being nominated for an honour meant that I was in the running for one, not that I was actually being given one. It amazed me when I realized, because I still felt so close to the beginning of my career and I'd always thought these honours were for lifetime achievements.

On the big day I took my parents and my brother with me to the Palace and tried to hide my nerves behind a Philip Treacey hat and a new suit. There were a crowd of us waiting to receive our honours and we were all made to practise our routine of bowing or curtseying to the Queen then walking backwards away from her. At least I was trained not to fall over.

The ceremony seemed to last for hours, yet when my turn finally came I was very impressed at how personal the Queen made it feel. Of course she had someone by her side reminding her in a very low voice of each person's name, but she didn't give any indication that this was a tedious job for her, and she chatted very pleasantly to me about some shows I had just danced, and some performances which were coming up. She'd been perfectly briefed and got every detail correct. But for weeks afterwards the company kept teasing me and calling me Dame Darcey Bussell.

7

Fans, Flowers – and Critics

SOMETIMES I CAN get so wrapped up in my daily routine that I forget there's a whole world out there for which I'm meant to be dancing, a world of fans and of critics. Yet of course the public's attitude to me is crucial. When audiences love a dancer it not only lifts his or her confidence, it also affects how they're treated by the company. It helps anyone's career to have the fans and critics on their side.

But I have to admit that I keep a wary distance from the critics. I was first reviewed when I danced the school performance of *Concerto* but even then I remember that what most concerned me was getting my photograph published in *The Dancing Times*. This magazine always features a lot of ballet photos and I couldn't wait for the new edition to come out, to see if there was a picture of me in it. At sixteen, getting my picture in print was my definition of fame. So it was only after I'd admired my photo in the magazine that I took a breath and nerved myself to read the review of the show. In fact the magazine's critic, Mary Clarke, wrote some very encouraging things about me, as did the newspaper critics who reviewed the performance. But they still didn't give me a taste for reading my own reviews and during all the years that I've danced with The Royal I've never deliberately bought the papers to look at what the critics say.

It's a habit that has partly grown out of self-defence. I've seen dancers who've been so devastated by bad reviews that they've not only lost faith in their work, but also stopped enjoying it. I love dancing and I don't want anything to spoil my pleasure in it. I also don't feel that I need the critics' comments. I get a lot of personal feedback and criticism from my coaches – who understand in detail the work I'm doing – and I'm my own harshest critic. I usually know what's wrong before anyone has told me, and I always prepare myself for the worst that anyone can say.

But I can't cut myself off from the critics completely. My mother clips all of my reviews and she shows me the ones she thinks will interest me – or rather the ones that she agrees with! I'll often read these a few days after the show, when I know they can't affect me. But I may also be shown a review by one of the other dancers and if we've just put on a new production, then word of what the reviews have been like spreads very fast. So it's impossible not to have a general idea of what is being written about me, and at the beginning of my career I did get very discouraged by it because so many critics were making negative comments about my youth and inexperience. They weren't arguing with my technique but with my acting ability and my grasp of certain roles. Of course I *was* very young to be dancing principal roles, but I resented them saying so.

In retrospect I have to admit they were often right. I was so caught up with the challenge of trying to perfect the choreography that I didn't always understand its dramatic and emotional richness. I still had to learn that the effect of a performance doesn't depend entirely on technique, so it's true that I have grown up into my repertoire.

But there are some complaints critics make which infuriate me because they're directed at things no one can change. With me it's often my height, while with other dancers it may be the size of their feet or even the shape of their body. Personal remarks like that are pointlessly hurtful. Critics should look at the way dancers interpret a role, not become fixated on their anatomy.

As a company we also get very resentful of the older critics who write obsessively about dancers who were performing forty years ago, comparing us all with Margot Fonteyn. Ballet has changed as an art form, and we're a new generation of dancers, so of course we have our own style. We're no worse than the older dancers, we're just different. Sometimes I wish we could have film footage of past generations running alongside us during performances so that we could say, 'Look. See, we are completely unlike them. Don't complain about the fact, write about what we're doing now.'

Some critics complain that ballet has become technically showy and has lost its dramatic expression, but again they write as if they haven't woken up to what the art form is like today. Physically, it's progressed so far that we can now do things with our bodies which were technically impossible for older dancers. Before she died, Margot often used to say that she doubted she'd be able to get a job in one of today's *corps de ballets*. Of course she would, but we can't help being affected by the physical range that we're capable of, and in certain ballets we like to show it off. It doesn't mean that we can't act or that we don't care about emotional nuance.

In terms of public reaction we probably listen, as a company, more to our audiences than to the critics these days. There's intense pressure on us to be entertaining and to fill the theatres, because money is short and we face so much competition from other companies, like Adventures in Motion Pictures, whose male version of *Swan Lake* ran for weeks in the West End in 1996. (I loved this production, it retained so much of the poetry of Petipa and Ivanov's original ballet even while it was so funny, and I loved the physicality of the male swans. Watching the way their muscles undulated in their bare backs gave me an image of the quality I aim for when I'm dancing Odette myself.) So if the critics carp about a new show but the audiences love it, we trust the public. When we first danced William Forsythe's ballet *In the middle, somewhat elevated* in 1991 it was slated by some of the press, but it sold so well there wasn't even standing room left in the theatre. Of course we continue to perform it.

Audiences may also be a more reliable test of a dancer's performance as well as of a new show. If I know that someone has been badly affected by a harsh review I'll always say to them, 'Come on, this is only one person's opinion. Did the audience boo you? No, they didn't, they clapped.'

We don't always feel that critics know what they are talking about. Some of the points on which they comment could be spotted by anyone in the audience – a bad mistake or a dancer being off form – and when some critics try to get technical they can be wrong. They may pass comments about the choreography which are simply inaccurate, or they may complain that a dancer is not performing a solo in a certain way, when in fact they haven't got the point of the choreography themselves.

When we read a review that's badly informed we do take revenge by passing it around and saying how ridiculous it is. We also feel that critics never know the company as well as they think they do. Sometimes they rave about the way a certain dancer performs a role – as if it's a definitive performance – but we know that there's a third or fourth cast dancer who actually does it better. If critics could come into rehearsals and see several dancers performing the same choreography, then they could really judge us.

But all the same we accept that critics are necessary, and of course it's wonderful when they give us praise. I always feel gratified when a critic notices that I've put a lot of work into a role and have really gone for it (though it's infuriating when I've killed myself in a show and haven't had any reaction at all). We also respect critics for the amount that they've seen, and if they comment on us having given a good performance in one of the classics it feels special, because we know they've seen so much else to compare us with.

Critics are also a useful outside eye. In a company we tend to get very accustomed to each other and we become blind to some of our faults as well as the good points in our work. Even coaches may stop making certain corrections, so a critic can jolt us into seeing ourselves afresh. They are also interesting to read when we perform new productions. As dancers we often feel very ambivalent about a new ballet. On the one hand we try to believe that every work we do is wonderful as we need to psyche ourselves up to give a good performance. On the other hand we may start to have doubts about the production and there comes a point when we start criticizing it to protect ourselves. If it's going to be a flop we don't want to think that it's our fault. So it's always interesting to test our views against those of the critics. And of course we're always desperate for good reviews because they affect ticket sales so much. It's very depressing to create a new ballet which doesn't sell, and which fizzles out of the repertoire after only a few performances. When you've put so much work into creating something you want it to be a success.

One of the most flattering reviews I ever received was in the *New York Times* – and it began, 'There are three good things about The Royal Ballet. Darcey Bussell, Darcey Bussell, and Darcey Bussell.' It was lovely for me, but I was cringing at how unfair it was to the rest of the company. Most of the other dancers fortunately thought it was very funny, but even so I'd rather read eulogies like that in the privacy of my own fan letters.

When I'm performing regularly at the Opera House I get a post bag of about ten or fifteen fan letters a week and I employ a very kind lady, Dorothy, once a fortnight to help me sort through them. Most of them are just requests for autographs, signed photographs or signed ballets shoes, but some ask for holiday photos which I won't give out and some send me whole questionnaires asking about my work and what my favourite ballets are. I dread these as they're such hard work.

The style of writing and the comments vary incredibly from letter to letter. A lot come from children – especially little girls – who basically say that they want to be me when they grow up! I had a charming one from an eleven-year-old called Vanessa Garwood who wrote to tell me that she did '*tons* of ballet' and wished she 'could be a dancer' like me. She said her letter had taken her 'nineteen days to write' as she'd 'been planning it in my head ever since I saw *The Nutcracker*. You were absolutely fantastic. If you have a spare moment to write back to me don't hesitate but I fully understand if you can't. (Being the prima ballerina is not easy!)'

It's nice when fans are so considerate. It's always very touching when people send me money to cover return postage when they request photographs and I have one fan, Wendy Glavis, who writes to me regularly from

Peterborough and who is always terribly concerned that I shouldn't feel under any obligation to reply. Her letters always end 'P.S. No reply expected'. In fact her own letters are amazingly long. Wendy is overwhelmingly positive about my work and takes a very detailed interest in it. She once wrote 'The end of May saw the fourth anniversary of the first time I saw you dance and I really must thank you again for all the pleasure and inspiration you've given me in that time.' But her compliments are accompanied by very precise commentary about performances – the way I held certain balances, the kind of tempi the conductor was using – and she also sends me gossip from the other fans. In the same letter she wrote, 'By the way, the conversation in the Friends (of Covent Garden) queue this morning was to the effect that *Don Quixote* is very much all right and the critics are idiots. Inside The Royal Opera House however the usherettes were busy discussing *you*. They were full of admiration (although slightly tinged with envy because *All the men like Darcey* but they weren't really holding it against you!).'

When I hear from fans like Wendy it obviously makes me feel that my work is worth something – and also when I hear from people like Darren Tansley, who wrote that watching me and the company had made him appreciate ballet for the first time. He'd always thought ballet 'was an elitist art form, performed for the benefit of a few rich and pretentious snobs,' but his 'preconceptions had been torn apart.'

One of the most heartbreaking letters I received was from a man who wrote to tell me that he'd seen me dancing *Swan*

Lake, 'something I will never forget as you were outstanding,' but 'as you can see by my address' would be unable to see my next show. It was from a prison in Lincolnshire.

A few letters reveal some very murky sexual fantasies, and of course I ignore those. But the more romantic letters I have to respond to, however uncomfortable they may make me feel. I got one letter from a man begging me for a lock of my hair the next time I went to the hairdresser, and a surprising number of men actually ask me to meet them. Nearly all of them *claim* that they've never done anything like this before and are not cranks and a few are dinner invitations from pilots in the RAF, which is especially odd as they admit they've never seen me dance. But apparently they've read a lot about me and they say they're going to be in London on leave and would love to take me out. It's all very flattering, it makes me feel like a Second World War pin-up.

Some requests come from men who've seen me on television and decide I am someone they need to get to know. One letter I received got positively poetic as the writer wound himself up to ask to see me: 'now as midnight chimes, Miles Davis plays, and the fire roars in the grate I am determined at least to try (to meet you)'. When I reply and say that I can't meet up with strangers, or when they hear that I have a husband, they claim they are distraught.

It's far less complicated when I get anonymous postcards such as the one which simply said, 'Dance for me tonight, xxx a mysterious dark stranger' or when fans send presents.

I am sent an amazing variety of things including little ballet ornaments like crystal swans, teddy bears, paintings and books that people think I will like. One of my most regular fans, Shirley, who is a school teacher, sent me a pair of point shoes made out of chocolate, which was lovely except that I'm not meant to eat chocolate.

Letters and presents like this naturally make me feel under an obligation to my fans and of course I'm grateful for their admiration and generosity. But it does take a lot of time to reply to everyone and some fans presume that I'm somehow always available to them. They believe I owe them a debt and that I would not be where I am but for them. They also seem to think that they know me intimately when really the person they are writing to is the image I project on stage. I once got a letter describing me as a creature 'who had stepped out of a fairy story, no mortal could be so lovely, so ethereal' and it's not me at all.

I feel uncomfortable knowing that there are people in the world who think they have a special claim on me and I'm nervous of the fact that there's now a Darcey Bussell website on the Internet, run by a group of fans who send each other gossip and information. I have no idea what they say about me and how much of it is true, but I certainly don't want to log on and find out. I know that some fans of Adam Cooper set up a website while he was starring in Adventures in Motion Picture's *Swan Lake* and for some reason a few of them started to give him the nickname Sheep. A whole secret cult of Adam fans developed who identified each other over the Net using the nickname.

But I do sympathize with fans who want some personal connection with dancers simply because they love the art form so much, and there's always a small crowd of those waiting outside the stage door after a show. Some of them I know quite well, like Shirley and her friend Jennifer, and a man called Ian who comes to most of my performances. Others are there for the first time and get very nervous when I speak to them. They overreact wildly and burst into hysterical laughter if I make the slightest joke.

That makes me feel self-conscious, but in Japan the crowds can make me feel plain scared. Ballet is very popular over there and the audiences are really fabulous, they give us standing ovations that last for twenty minutes, and they have to be thrown out of the theatre. But after the show hundreds of them swarm round to the stage door so when we come out of the theatre there are people everywhere and cameras flashing. It's like being a pop star but it's physically very frightening. Everyone is jostling us so hard that we have trouble getting through.

Other fans just send flowers, which I love, although it can be very uncomfortable when we get to the end of a show and some dancers are laden down with flowers and others are standing there empty-handed. This gives out very misleading signals to the audience, most of whom tend to assume that if a dancer is presented with lavish bouquets she's given a particularly wonderful performance. In fact a dancer who only received one tiny bunch may have danced much better. I remember as a student I was always over-impressed by dancers' flowers. I'd describe a show that a ballerina had performed and sigh, 'And she got the most beautiful flowers' – as if that was the crucial point.

I should have known better, yet the ballerina-garlanded-with-flowers is so much part of the art form's image. It's so essential that some of the world's most famous ballerinas will often send bouquets to themselves, to make sure they have flowers at the end of a show. If a star dancer is making a brief guest appearance in a foreign city she can't run the risk of not getting any floral tributes at the end of a show as it would look as if she'd somehow failed. I'm very fortunate because my mother, who is my biggest fan, sends me flowers after every show. She buys them at trade price at Covent Garden market. But few of the other dancers in the company have such a reliable source.

I also used to get regular flowers from a fan called Sam and I'd always know which were from him because there would be a Kit Kat tucked into them. The flowers were beautiful but having a Kit Kat at the end of a show was the real treat. I have an American fan called Alan too, who travels around the world on business and whenever he ends up in a city where I'm performing he always sends me sixteen red roses. Whenever I see them, I know Alan's in town.

In our company the stage management are fortunately careful about sharing out flowers at the end of a show, so that if some of the principals have been sent a lot and others have none they're distributed equally at curtain calls. (We get them back afterwards of course and I always read through the cards before I leave so that I can thank people at the stage door.) If I have a very busy week when I'm doing several shows then I may end up with more flowers than I can fit into my house. Some I give away to my partner – Johnny especially likes to take some home – and I give a lot to my local hospital.

At the end of gala evenings we often have flowers hurled down at us from the boxes, which gets very exciting though we have to be careful taking curtain calls as squashed stems are so slippery. I've taken bows too where I've noticed the other dancers have been falling about with laughter and I've realized that I had a flower stalk sticking up from my headdress.

Sometimes people throw flowers from the front stalls, which they weight with Plasticine to get a better aim. These can really hurt if they hit your leg. It can also be awkward not knowing who they're intended for – I've sometimes bent down to pick some up and then seen a little face in the audience looking frantic because they were meant for another dancer.

During the curtain calls – which we call red runners as the curtain is only slightly drawn back – I always like the fact that we can see the audience for the first time. It gives us a much more intimate connection with them (although we're always at the mercy of the stage management who some-times don't pull the curtains back when we want to come out, or sometimes do when we don't!). They also allow us, if we have enough of them, to unfreeze from our roles as we bow. If I've danced a ballet like *Romeo and Juliet* or *Giselle* which has been very emotionally draining, I'm still in character when I take my first couple of bows. After dancing Juliet's death, I physically cannot make myself smile or look normal. It's only after a few minutes that I become myself.

When I guested with the Kirov in St Petersburg I discovered that they had very strict rules for taking curtain calls. The ballerina isn't allowed to put down her own flowers when she walks forward to bow, her partner has to take them from her, nor is she allowed to bow on her own, she always has to be presented to the audience by her man.

Of course the Russians also have a wonderfully elaborate style of bowing and I've always loved the way that Sylvie takes her calls too, she stands for ages just looking at the audience before she finally bows. Everyone has to develop their own style and if the calls go on and on we have to find ways of varying what we do – we may walk to the edges of the stage and bow to other parts of the theatre or the man may spin the woman across him with a little flourish. It can get a bit mannered sometimes – I think if we videoed our performances we might be shocked at some of the things we do on stage. And the most embarrassing of them all is when dancers don't judge the applause accurately. They continue bowing as the clapping is fading away, then have to leave the stage in dead silence. At moments like that everyone feels like running, but you have to keep your dignity and walk off slowly.

Even though I'm barely conscious of the audience while I'm dancing it's always important to me to know that some of my friends and family are watching. My mother comes to all my performances – she must have sat through fifty

Sleeping Beauties by now – and Angus always comes on a first night. There are usually a few of my friends as well as some regular fans in the theatre plus a couple of our sponsors, Ben and Christine, who I know, who regularly sit in the same place. So I always have a sense of where my support is coming from in the auditorium and I can rely on some people to give me a good clap.

Applause is obviously wonderful for my ego, but it also influences my standing in the company. It helps, naturally, when the management think we are really popular. So if ever I know that a lot of my friends or family are coming to a performance I always beg them to bring their football rattles!

CODA

BALLET IS AN odd career. It is glamorous, magical and inspiring but at the same time it is also grindingly hard, and precarious work, and most dancers today have adopted a much more practical approach to their art than previous generations. We struggle every day to create illusions on stage and yet we have to be total pragmatists.

One aspect of the profession about which we've had to become most realistic is the competition we face, not only from within ballet itself but also from other forms of entertainment. Even though we believe passionately in the value of our own art form we can no longer remain wrapped up in its values. There is no point perfecting our technique and making new ballets unless the public come to see us, and unless at least some of the work endures.

So while we are always hungry to create new ballets we do worry whether they will sell well at the box office. Some dancers get frustrated and ask why we don't just put on musicals – as that's what the public seem to want. I try to think of all the new productions Diaghilev staged, which were very controversial at the time but are now seen as classics, but with each new work the company – and the dancers – take a risk. When Johnny and I first danced *Pavane*, we were very anxious about how it would go down with the public. The choreography is very classical and it has a quiet, dreamy quality which we weren't sure audiences would respond to. It was so gratifying when they loved it so much.

I'm sure that today's dancers also experience more pressure from within the profession than previous generations. During the '60s, Balanchine created a vogue for tall, beautiful ballerinas in his own company, New York City Ballet, and that image has now spread everywhere so that we've become hypercritical of our own and each other's appearances. We all want to have long skinny legs, a long neck and fabulously arched feet, which means that some dancers who may actually move across the stage beautifully, who may be great dance actresses or have a charismatic personality don't get the appreciation they deserve. They may fail to get a role that suits them perfectly because they don't look good in the costume. Sometimes it seems that we judge dancers not as performers, but as a collection of body parts.

Ballet technique has also become so much more athletic that we can no longer get by on a natural talent for dancing or a glamorous image. Dancers maintain an intensive physical regime in which the traditional routine of daily class and rehearsal is no longer enough. We go to the gym regularly, do Pilates training to condition our muscles and we have very hi-tech methods for dealing with stress and injury. We also swim or cycle to build up our stamina and I wonder how many of the public would continue to think of us as princesses and princes if they saw the women pedalling away on their exercise bikes or the men lifting weights. It changes the image somewhat.

Since ballet has become so physically demanding, none of us can conceive of having the long careers which older ballerinas like Margot Fonteyn, Alicia Markova or Natasha Makarova enjoyed. Our bodies couldn't cope, and this is another reason why my generation seems to view our art in a less romantic light. We have to think hard about whether we want to have children while we are still performing, and we have to be aware of what we might do as a second career. The injury rate has also become higher so more dancers are aware that their career might be ended at any moment. We are very conscious now of the toll that ballet takes on our bodies in later life. Do we really want to struggle on dancing into our late thirties and forties when we may end up with two false hips as a result?

At twenty-nine I am already beginning to consider all this. I have promised myself that I will try and retire gracefully – at the peak of my career rather than when it has started to slide – and I guess this will be when I'm about thirty-five. But it's never possible to predict. As dancers we can often experience a new lease of life when we least expect it, so if I feel inspired I may carry on a little longer.

Yet I doubt I would survive until I was forty because I'm so hypercritical of myself, and it would make me miserable to perform below my best. There are also so many other things I want to do. I want to have children, and I'm interested in the possibility of taking courses in interior or theatre design. I'd like to try myself out as an actress although I don't want to re-create the pressures I'm under as a dancer. What I really look forward to most is having a normal life.

Hopefully though I still have several years of this strange, addictive profession in front of me and while I am dancing I'm conscious of maximizing my work and not wasting a minute of my performing life. I'm hungrier for work now than when I first started. I'm still driven by a need to improve and I still crave new roles. Much as I like the classics and much as I know the public love them, I feel that I'm repeating myself if I dance these ballets too often. Without new roles to dance, the inspiration is harder and harder to find.

At The Royal we have an unusually large repertory so we *are* given a wide range of roles to dance, but even so we tend to concentrate on the best-selling works and there are many neglected ballets which I'd jump at the chance to perform. I can feel the minutes ticking past and I don't want to devote them all to *Sleeping Beauty* and *Swan Lake* (of course I'm lucky to be able to organize guest appearances outside the company and I do feel badly for those who have fewer chances. The whole company need to be fulfilled, not just the box office stars).

But even if we dancers have had to become more hard-headed about our careers, and our public image has become less mysterious, ballet itself has lost none of its magic. It is still such a rich and potent spectacle. When I was a child I fell in love with the jewellery, the costumes, the lighting, the music and the whole stage design as well as becoming passionate about the dance itself. And all those elements are still there. As we sweat and curse on stage, however cynically we may complain, our reason for being there is still to ensure that when the lights go down, the orchestra starts and the curtains open, the audience feel shivers running down their spines.

CHRONOLOGY OF DÉBUTS
IN MAJOR ROLES WITH
THE ROYAL BALLET

All performances are at The Royal Opera House unless otherwise specified.

17 November 1988	Lilac Fairy in Petipa's *The Sleeping Beauty*
22 November 1988	**Created** principal role in Bintley's *Spirit of Fugue*
31 December 1988	Winter Fairy in Ashton's *Cinderella*
14 March 1989	Soloist in Balanchine's *Capriccio (Rubies)*
17 March 1989	Lady Mary in Ashton's *Enigma Variations*

14 April 1989	Swan in Petipa and Ivanov's *Swan Lake*
18 May 1989	Second Solo Shade in Petipa's *La Bayadère*
27 May 1989	Gamzatti in Petipa's *La Bayadère*
12 October 1989	Agnus Dei role in MacMillan's *Requiem*
7 December 1989	**Created** role of Princess Rose in MacMillan's *The Prince of the Pagodas*
26 January 1990	Lead female role in Chaboukiani's *Laurentia*
3 February 1990	Odette/Odile in Petipa and Ivanov's *Swan Lake*
21 April 1990	Myrtha in Perrot/Coralli/Petipa's *Giselle*
28 April 1990	*Pas de Deux* in Bintley's *Galanteries*
28 April 1990	*Pas de Deux* in Ashley Page's *Pursuit*
17 May 1990	White woman in MacMillan's *Song of the Earth*
July 1990	**Created** female role in MacMillan's *Farewell Pas de Deux* at The Palladium (then at the Royal Opera House 1 August 1990)
26 October 1990	Bethena Waltz in MacMillan's *Elite Syncopations*
29 November 1990	Aria 1 Woman in Balanchine's *Stravinsky Violin Concerto*
29 November 1990	**Created** role in Brown trio in Page's *Bloodlines*
1 December 1990	Raymonda in Petipa's *Raymonda*

26 December 1990	Sugar Plum Fairy in Ivanov's *The Nutcracker*
7 February 1991	**Created** role of Masha in MacMillan's *Winter Dreams*
10 April 1991	*Pas de Deux* in Balanchine's *Agon*
5 June 1991	Hostess in Nijinska's *Les Biches*
4 November 1991	Woman in Balanchine's *Tchaikovsky Pas de Deux*
20 November 1991	Lead roles in Tuckett's *Present Histories*
3 December 1991	Ballerina in the second movement of Balanchine's *Symphony in C*
13 February 1992	Principal woman in Forsythe's *In the middle, somewhat elevated*
17 February 1992	Principal woman in Ashton's *Trois Gymnopédies/Monotones*
29 February 1992	Manon in MacMillan's *Manon*
17 May 1992	Nikiya in Petipa's *La Bayadère*, Tokyo (then at The Royal Opera House 31 March 1997)
29 October 1992	Mitzi Caspar in MacMillan's *Mayerling*
4 January 1993	Cinderella in Ashton's *Cinderella*
12 January 1993	Terpsichore in Balanchine's *Apollo*
30 January 1993	Aurora in Petipa's *The Sleeping Beauty*
30 April 1993	*Pas de Trois* in Balanchine's *Ballet Imperial*
4 June 1993	The Prostitute in Tetley's *La Ronde*
4 June 1993	Black Queen in de Valois' *Checkmate*
5 June 1993	The Siren in Balanchine's *Prodigal Son*
30 October 1993	Juliet in MacMillan's *Romeo and Juliet*

24 November 1993	*Pas de Deux* in Forsythe's *Herman Schmerman*
15 December 1993	*Pas de Deux* in Balanchine's *Ballet Imperial*
9 December 1994	Principal woman in Ashton's *Raymonda pas de deux*
25 January 1995	Principal woman in Balanchine's *Duo Concertant* in Dance Bites tour (then at The Royal Opera House 6 April 1995)
20 May 1995	Giselle in Perrot/Coralli/Petipa's *Giselle* at Sejong (then at The Royal Opera House 26 July 1995)
9 December 1995	**Created** role of Truth on Toe in Tharp's *Mr Worldly Wise*
7 February 1996	**Created** role in Matthew Hart's *Dances with Death*
19 March 1996	Principal woman in Page's . . . *now languorous, now wild* . . . in Dance Bites tour
15 April 1996	Sacred Love in Ashton's *Illuminations*
3 May 1996	Kschessinska in MacMillan's *Anastasia*
18 October 1996	**Created** principal woman role in Wheeldon's *Pavane pour une infante défunte*
13 February 1997	Principal female (Van Hamel) role in Tharp's *Push Comes to Shove*
30 April 1997	**Created** role in Tetley's *Amores*

| 15 June 1998 | Beriosova solo in Ashton's *Birthday Offering* at Barbican |
| 19 June 1998 | Fonteyn *Pas de Deux* in Ashton's *Birthday Offering* at Barbican |

GLOSSARY OF NAMES AND DANCE TERMS

Adage or Adagio Any slow dance movement – as opposed to fast or allegro movements. It also refers to the central section of a class in which the dancers develop their balance and line, and to the first section of a *pas de deux*. See **Rose Adage**.

Adventures in Motion Pictures London-based modern dance theatre company founded in 1987 and directed by Matthew Bourne. It scored a huge popular success in 1995 with Bourne's updated version of *Swan Lake*, in which all the swans were danced by men, and also with his 1997 setting of Prokofiev's Cinderella, in which the story was relocated to wartime London.

American Ballet Theatre   New York-based ballet company founded in 1940 which performs a mixed repertory of classics and twentieth-century ballets. Many of the world's greatest dancers have appeared as guest stars.

Arabesque   One of the fundamental positions in classical ballet in which the dancer stands on one leg, with the other extended into the air behind, creating the image of a line stretched tight between the tips of the dancer's fingers and toes. Traditionally, the back leg is raised to ninety degrees from the ground with the torso remaining upright, although the leg may sometimes be lifted and in an arabesque *penché* the dancer tilts the torso towards the floor, so bringing the leg up higher.

Ashton, Sir Frederick (1904–1988)   One of Britain's greatest classical choreographers. During much of his career he was chief choreographer of The Royal Ballet (and its director from 1963 to 1970), and his many ballets helped evolve the company's distinctively elegant and lyrical style as well as developing the career of his muse, Margot Fonteyn. Among his best-known works are *Cinderella* (1948), *La Fille mal gardée* (1960) and *The Dream* (1964).

Attitude   A position in classical ballet where the dancer stands on one leg and raises the other to the front, side, or back with the knee bent to an angle of around ninety degrees.

Balanchine, George (1904–1983)   The Russian choreographer who became one of the defining architects of American ballet. He danced in St Petersburg during the post-revolutionary period, with the company formerly known as The Maryinsky Ballet, and later known as The Kirov, then in 1924 left to join Diaghilev's Ballets Russes where he choreographed his seminal work *Apollo musagète* (1928). In 1933 he moved to America where with Lincoln Kerstein he founded New York City Ballet. He choreographed many ballets, in which he developed his version of neo-classicism streamlining the ballet vocabulary and bringing to it a modern speed and attack. These include *Serenade* (1934), *Symphony in C* (1947), *Agon* (1957) and *Jewels* (1967).

ballet master or mistress   The men and women who are responsible for rehearsing ballets after they have been choreographed.

barre   The wooden rail running at about waist height along the walls of a dance studio, which the dancers hold to stabilize their balance while they are performing exercises during the beginning of class.

Beriosova, Svetlana   Born in Lithuania in 1932, she was the daughter of the famous ballet master Nicholas Beriozoff. She was a soloist with Sadler's Wells Theatre Ballet and transferred to The Royal Ballet (or Sadler's Wells Ballet as it was still then called) in 1952, where she became a ballerina in

1955. Her best-known roles included Odette/Odile and Swanilda. She retired from the stage in 1975.

Bintley, David   British choreographer, born in 1957. He joined Sadler's Wells Royal Ballet in 1976 where he began to choreograph in 1978. His ballets include *Spirit of Fugue* (1988), *Hobson's Choice* (1989) and *Edward II* (1995). He became director of Birmingham Royal Ballet in 1995.

bourrée   Fast running step, performed in any direction, in which the dancer appears to almost glide over the surface of the stage.

Carabosse   The evil fairy in Petipa's *Sleeping Beauty* who lays a curse on the Princess Aurora. Depending on the production the role may be performed by either a man or a woman.

chaîné turns   A sequence of fast seamless turns in which the dancer moves from one foot to another.

chassée   Ballet step in which the dancer slides the foot in any direction, keeping the heel on the floor and bending one or both knees.

coda   The final section in a classical *pas de deux*, performed by the ballerina and her partner. See also *pas de deux*.

corps de ballet   The male and female dancers in a ballet

company who perform together as a group, as opposed to the soloists and principals. They are the equivalent of the chorus in opera and, in the nineteenth-century classics especially, are choreographed to form abstract decorative patterns which provide visual or dramatic interludes to the main action.

Dance Theatre of Harlem   American ballet company founded by Arthur Mitchell in 1971 to nurture the careers of black dancers.

développé   An unfolding movement of the leg to the front, side or back, which displays the dancer's flexibility, strength and control.

Diaghilev, Sergei (1872–1929)   Russian impresario who founded Les Ballets Russes – the company which dominated European ballet between 1909 and 1929. He worked with young experimental choreographers like Fokine, Nijinsky, Nijinska, Massine and Balanchine, and collaborated with some of the most avant-garde painters and composers of the era, including Picasso, Satie and De Chirico.

Dowell, Sir Anthony   Born in 1943, he became one of the greatest classical male dancers in Britain. He trained at The Royal Ballet School and joined The Royal Ballet in 1961 where he was promoted to principal in 1966. Renowned for his lightness and fluency, he danced all the classic roles and was also well-known as Oberon in Ashton's *The Dream* and

Des Grieux in MacMillan's *Manon*. He has been director of
The Royal Ballet since 1986.

enchaînement   A sequence of linked ballet steps.

floor cloth   The cloth covering the stage for dance performances, painted or treated in accordance with the design
of the individual ballet.

Fonteyn, Dame Margot (1919–1991)   The prima ballerina
assoluta of The Royal Ballet. She trained at the Sadler's Wells
School and joined the company in 1934, becoming principal
in 1935. She was famous for her musicality and elegance and
for her ability to touch her audience's hearts, and she not
only danced all the classic ballerina roles but also created
roles in many works including Ashton's *Symphonic
Variations, Birthday Offering* and *Ondine*. Her partnership
with Nureyev turned her into an international star, as they
danced together in works like MacMillan's *Romeo and Juliet*
and Ashton's *Marguerite and Armand*. Her last role was in
Ronald Hynd's *The Merry Widow* in 1976 for the Australian
Ballet, marking a career that lasted over forty years.

fouetté   A fast turn in which the stretched working leg is
whipped from the front out to the side and then angled back
in at the knee as the dancer turns. It is usually performed in
series – as in the thirty-two *fouettés* in Act III of *Swan Lake*.

Grey, Dame Beryl   Born in 1927, she joined Sadler's Wells

Ballet as its youngest dancer in 1941 and danced Odette/Odile a year later. An unusually tall dancer for her generation with a very strong technique, she created roles in many ballets, including Ashton's *Cinderella* and *Birthday Offering*. After leaving The Royal to dance freelance she was artistic director of London Festival Ballet from 1968 to 1979.

Guillem, Sylvie Born in 1965, she studied at the Paris Opéra Ballet School and joined the company in 1981 where she was promoted to *étoile* in 1984, In 1989 she joined The Royal Ballet as principal guest artist and also dances freelance. She is a dancer of unique flexibility and control, with a charismatic stage personality.

Ivanov, Lev (1834–1901) The Russian choreographer who choreographed Acts II and IV of the famous 1895 version of *Swan Lake* (Petipa choreographed Acts I and III) as well as *The Nutcracker* in 1892. He worked as ballet master at The Maryinsky Theatre in St Petersburg.

jeté A jump from one foot to another in which the working leg appears to be thrown into the air, either forwards, backwards or sideways. There are many variations of this jump; in a *grand jeté* the dancer leaps as high and as far as possible, with both legs stretched to form the splits position at the apex of the jump.

Kirkland, Gelsey Born in 1952, she joined New York City Ballet in 1968, becoming principal in 1972. In 1974 she joined American Ballet Theatre where she danced regularly with both Mikhail Baryshnikov and Rudolf Nureyev. A rigorous perfectionist with a powerful dramatic talent, her performances were celebrated for their unique intensity and lyricism. She published her autobiography *Dancing on My Grave* in 1986.

Kirov Ballet, The St Petersburg ballet company which dates back to a dance school founded in 1783. It has variously been known as The Imperial Ballet, The Maryinsky Ballet, GATOB and The Kirov Ballet and in Russia has reverted to the name Maryinsky. The company reached a peak during the nineteenth century when Petipa was choreographing his enormous repertory of works and many of the world's greatest ballerinas were dancing with it. It is still regarded as a treasure-house of classical dance though it lacks a significant modern repertoire.

MacLeary, Donald Born in 1937, he trained at the Sadler's Wells School and by 1959 was principal dancer with The Royal Ballet. He was Beriosova's favourite partner and created roles in many ballets including MacMillan's *Le Baiser de la Fée*. Since 1984 he has coached the principal dancers in the company.

MacMillan, Sir Kenneth (1929-1992) Regarded, with Ashton, as one of Britain's greatest classical choreographers. He trained at the Sadler's Wells School and joined Sadler's Wells Theatre Ballet in 1946, He created his first professional ballet in 1953 and between 1977 and 1992 was The Royal Ballet's principal choreographer. His many ballets include *Romeo and Juliet* (1965), *Manon* (1974) and *Requiem* (1977) and though some of his works dealt with pure classical dance he was most famous for creating dance dramas whose psychological penetration and often painful subject matter extended the traditional boundaries of ballet.

Makarova, Natalia (Natasha)   Born in 1940, she danced with The Kirov as one of its leading ballerinas until she defected to the West in 1970. Here she became the most internationally famous ballerina of her generation, performing most frequently with American Ballet Theatre and also guesting with The Royal Ballet. With her extravagant line and dramatic intensity her range extended from Giselle to Manon. She staged her own production of *La Bayadère* for American Ballet Theatre in 1980 (mounted by The Royal 1989).

Mason, Monica   Born in 1941, she studied at The Royal Ballet School and joined the company in 1958 where she became a principal in 1967. She created roles in several MacMillan ballets including his *Sacre du printemps* (1962) and has been coaching dancers in the company since 1984. She is now assistant artistic director.

Mukhamedov, Irek   Born in 1960, he studied at the Moscow Choreographic School and became one of the leading stars of The Bolshoi Ballet during the 1980s. His best-known role was

Spartacus, which showed off the extraordinary height and power of his jump as well as his ardent acting style. He left Russia and joined The Royal Ballet in 1990 where he has created roles in MacMillan's *Winter Dreams* and *The Judas Tree*.

New York City Ballet   New York-based ballet company founded in 1948. Its repertory is dominated by the work of George Balanchine, though it also has many ballets by Jerome Robbins, and it is renowned for the fast, athletic style of its dancers.

Nureyev, Rudolf (1938–1993)   The Russian dancer who formed an internationally famous partnership with Fonteyn, and became a ballet legend even during his own lifetime. He started ballet training late but was accepted into the Vaganova School in Leningrad and between 1958 and 1961 was one of the rising stars of The Kirov Ballet. After defecting to the West he joined The Royal Ballet as a permanent guest artist and began his long association with Fonteyn, astounding audiences with his charismatic personality and impetuous dance attack. He also pursued an exhausting freelance career in which he experimented with modern as well as classical dance (even acting in the musical *The King and I* in 1989). He was director of the Paris Opéra between 1983 and 1989 and he continued performing until two years before his death.

Paris Opéra   Paris-based ballet company which dates back to the *Académie royale de danse*, founded in 1661. It showcased stars like Marie Sallé and Gaetano Vestris in the eighteenth century and was home to the emergent Romantic ballet in the 1830s. In 1867 it moved to its present base, Palais Garnier, and today is renowned for the rigorous standard of its dancers and its varied repertory of classical and experimental ballet.

pas de deux This term can be used to describe any dance for two people but in Petipa's ballets the *pas de deux* were structured according to a strict formula. They opened with the ballerina and her partner dancing together, continued with each dancer performing a solo of their own, and concluded with a coda in which both danced together. They always featured highly acrobatic and elaborate choreography and, today, they are often danced in isolation from the rest of the ballet as gala items, eg the *Don Quixote pas de deux*.

Pavlova, Anna (1881–1931) The Russian ballerina who, during her extensive world tours, brought ballet to a world-wide audience and became the most famous dancer of her era. She danced with The Maryinsky Ballet, St Petersburg from 1899 until 1913 and danced briefly with Diaghilev's Ballets Russes before forming her own company. Though the ballets she performed were often trivial, the poetry of her own dancing inspired and enchanted audiences around the world. Her signature ballet was the brief solo Fokine choreographed specially for her, The Dying Swan.

Petipa, Marius (1818–1910) The French choreographer whose work elevated nineteenth-century ballet to its peak of beauty and sophistication. He studied with his father Jean Antoine Petipa, moved to St Petersburg in 1847 where he was a principal dancer, and created his first ballet in 1855. During his career he choreographed over fifty works including *Don Quixote* (1869) *La Bayadère* (1877), *The Sleeping Beauty* (1890) and *Raymonda* (1898) as well as *Swan Lake* with Ivanov in 1895.

pirouette   The word is French for spinning top and describes one or more turns performed while the dancer is balanced on point or half point (ie not fully on the tips of the toes). It can be performed with the working leg in several positions, stretched or bent at the knee.

plié From the French word *plier* (to bend), this term is used to describe the bending of the dancer's legs at the ankle and knee. A soft, deep *plié* is essential for the beginning and ending of all jumps and at the beginning of class, dancers warm up their leg muscles and joints with *plié* exercises.

point, on Dancing that is performed on the tips of the toes, while the dancer is wearing point shoes.

promenade   A slow turn performed while the dancer is balanced on one foot and holding a set pose (eg an arabesque or attitude) throughout. It can be executed solo, but during a *pas de deux* the ballerina's partner may hold her hand and turn her as she balances on point.

rond de jambe Movement where the dancer traces a semicircle with the leg, either from the front round to the back, or the back round to the front. It can be performed with the foot resting on the ground (*à terre*) or in the air (*en l'air*).

Rose Adage or Adagio Dance performed by Aurora and her four suitors in Act I of *The Sleeping Beauty*.

Royal Ballet, The Britain's largest ballet company. It was founded in 1931 by Ninette de Valois as The Vic Wells Ballet, performing both at the Sadler's Wells Theatre and The Old Vic. It changed its name to Sadler's Wells Ballet and in 1946 moved its performing base to the Opera House, Covent Garden (though for many years the company's offices and rehearsal studios were at their headquarters in Baron's Court). At this point a second touring company was created, with a London base at Sadler's Wells. This was initially called Sadler's Wells Opera Ballet, but soon became known as Sadler's Wells Theatre Ballet. In 1956 the resident Opera House company became known as The Royal Ballet and though for a while the second touring company was merged with The Royal, the companies separated again in 1975, with the Sadler's Wells Royal Ballet becoming Birmingham Royal Ballet in 1990 when it moved to its new base at The Birmingham Hippodrome.

shellac A thin glue used in the making of the hard end of point shoes.

Sibley, Dame Antoinette Born in 1939, she studied at

Sadler's Wells School and joined Sadler's Wells Ballet in 1956, becoming principal in 1960. A dancer of exquisite musicality and elegance, she danced all the classic ballerina roles and also created roles in Ashton's *The Dream* and MacMillan's *Manon*. She and Dowell formed an internationally famous partnership. She finally retired from the stage in the mid 1980s but still coaches on an occasional basis.

Tetley, Glen Born in 1926, he studied modern and classical dance in America and performed in several companies there (including Martha Graham's) before joining Nederlands Dans Theater in 1962 as dancer and choreographer. His early works were purely modern in style but over the years have become infused with more classical elements. His large output includes *Ricercare* (1966), *Voluntaries* (1973), *The Tempest* (1979) and *La Ronde* (1987).

Tharp, Twyla Born in 1942, she studied ballet and modern dance and performed with Paul Taylor's company before forming her own group. Her style has moved from austere modernism to a fusion of modern, classical and vernacular dance. She created *Push Comes to Shove* as a showcase for Mikhail Baryshnikov in 1976 and her other works include *In The Upper Room* (1986).

tutu The stiff layered skirt worn by ballerinas. In the nineteenth century this was worn at knee length but the modern tutu skims the dancer's upper thighs, acting as a frame for the action of her legs.

Valois, Dame Ninette de Born in 1898, she was the founder of The Royal Ballet. She danced with Diaghilev's Ballets Russes from 1923 to 1925 then on her return to London she established her own choreographic academy in 1926. In 1931 she formed the Vic Wells Ballet which was the foundation of both Royal Ballet companies. She choreographed several ballets, including *The Rake's Progress* (1935) and *Checkmate* (1937), and though she officially retired as director of The Royal Ballet in 1963 she was still an active presence both in the company and its school for many years.

Wright, Peter Born in 1926, he danced with several ballet companies before joining Sadler's Wells Theatre Ballet in 1949. He became ballet master there and also choreographed several ballets. In 1975 he became director of Sadler's Wells Royal Ballet (later Birmingham Royal Ballet) where he staged several renowned productions of the nineteenth-century classics.

Zelensky, Igor He trained at the Vaganova School in St Petersburg and danced with the Kirov Ballet until 1990, after which he danced with Berlin Ballet and New York City Ballet. Since 1997 he has danced freelance though he continues to guest regularly with New York City Ballet and The Kirov as well as with The Royal Ballet. He is celebrated for his high, graceful jump and effortless-looking pirouettes.